D1636633

RuM

THE
COMPLETE GUIDE
RUM

ISABEL BOONS AND TOM NEIJENS

LANNOO

"There's naught, no doubt, so much the spirit calms as rum and true religion."

Lord Byron

FOREWORD

"Life is more fun with rum!"

There is no other spirit that can be as rebellious as rum. It doesn't care about rules, doesn't like to be ordered about and always does its own thing. It's no wonder that this daredevil managed to win our hearts! And speaking of winning...

Does rum conjure up nostalgic childhood images for you too? Not images of binge drinking, of course, rather pictures of tough pirates braving rough seas with a glass of rum in their hand. Who didn't dream of being a real pirate, navigating the stormy seas to fight the enemy? And although pirates gradually lost that heroic status, a glass of rum still always lets us daydream about a life full of danger. Deep inside we all still want to be the rebel who is admired by everyone. That's probably exactly why rum fits so perfectly in a world that is full of adventure. Rum never gets boring: it challenges us and keeps on amazing us. Yes, that's right: *Life is more fun with rum!*

Since its creation, rum has not only tended to join the rebels, it has also introduced the term 'globalisation' to the world. The very least we can say is that the history of rum may be the most bloodcurdling of all the spirits. We will be dealing with this later in the book, when we will board pirate ships on our way to the most exotic of locations! After that, we will dive into the various production methods and look at the fascinating maturation process. The concept of 'rum' covers a wealth of colours, aromas and flavours that can be totally different every time you open a bottle: accessible or complex, soft or robust. Rum can turn from a predictable adolescent into a seasoned hedonist, while still remaining loyal to its rebellious character. It is almost impossible to group rums together under a single heading, but we have tried to classify them as well as possible in this book as a way of giving you some kind of guide. We have positioned fifty selected rums in our detailed Flavour Star and unleashed our selection of premium rums on you. After that, we will start tasting, both neat and in cocktails, but always with rum as the protagonist. Finally we will enjoy the nightlife, doubling up our pleasure... with both rum and cigars.

This book takes you on a stormy adventure to some of the most inhospitable locations in the world. It is an ode to a rebel, so we feel it is appropriate to end with the words of another rebel who died while this book was being written: David Bowie. *"Hot tramp, I love you so!"*

Ahoy matey and cheers!
Isabel Boons and Tom Neijens

WHAT IS RUM?

REBEL WITHOUT A CAUSE

You could say that rum is the rebel among the spirits: no rules, no laws and no prescribed definitions. Rum is subject mainly to the laws and rules of the country of origin. Rum from Columbia, for instance, has to have a minimum alcohol content of 50%, whereas countries such as Venezuela and Chile prescribe an alcohol content of only 40%. Mexico requires maturation for at least eight months, rum from the Dominican Republic must mature for at least one year, while Venezuela requires maturation for two years. There is also a difference in the nomenclature for the various types of rum. In the United States, for instance, rum is classified as 'rum', 'rum liquor' and 'flavored rum', whereas Barbados refers to rum as 'white rum', 'overproof rum' and 'matured rum'.

The age on the bottle label does not usually mean a lot. The age stated on the label of a whisky is that of

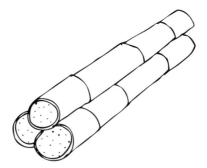

the youngest whisky in the bottle, but the age stated on the label of a rum refers to the oldest type in the bottle, even if just a drop is present. This looseness can be seen as both positive and negative. If offers a lot of opportunities for creativeness, but no guarantee that the quality of the content is high. Of course, in this book we're only dealing with rum that we are certain is high quality.

The description of rum tells us that it is a fermented and distilled spirit, made from the by-products of sugar cane, such as *molasses* (sticky syrup, the residue of sugar processing – see also 'Production process') and sugar cane sap. The distillate is usually matured in oak or other barrels. Rum is made almost anywhere that sugar cane grows, but the greatest production of rum is around the Caribbean and along the Demerara river in South America.

STYLES

Rum is produced in a lot of styles. If we rely only on the colour, we can classify it into two types: white rum and brown or dark rum. White rum is mainly used as a mixer, but

that doesn't mean that white rum can't taste fantastic. Dark rum derives its colour either from the barrels in which it is matured or from caramel-coloured additives. Spiced rums – in which all kinds of herbs are added to rum types, as the name suggests – mostly have a darker colour. However, we should emphasise that darker rum is no guarantee of high quality. Classifying rum on the basis of colour is undoubtedly an oversimplification. Classifying rum into various categories is not easy as there is no general standard for the ingredients, the production and the maturation, which creates a certain amount of chaos. Nevertheless, we can divide rum into categories despite the differences, namely by looking at the country of origin. Rum can be subdivided into three major categories: English, Spanish and French. This classification goes back to colonial times. The original populace of the rum-producing countries learned how to make liquor from their English, French or Spanish colonists. And the style does indeed refer to the language that is spoken today in the country of origin. But rum would not be rum if there were no outsiders. They will be discussed extensively later in the book, of course (see also 'Classification') and we will be your guide in the rebellious world of our much-beloved spirit. *But first things first...*

THE ORIGIN OF THE NAME 'RUM'

The exact origin of the name 'rum' is still a mystery to this day. Some people claim that *rumbullion* (a slang term for disturbances during the time of the pirates) is the origin of the word, while others suggest that rum was an old English word for 'excellent' (*having a rum time*). And the Latin name for sugar cane, *Saccharum*, is also seen by many as the explanation of the name 'rum'. Even the Dutch word *roemer* (a drinking glass or mug) has been suggested as the origin of the word. However, historians seem to agree that Barbados was the first location where drinks based on sugar cane were called *rumbullion*, alias *kill-devil*. The origin of the word may therefore perhaps be in the old slang word *rumbullion*.

A BRIEF HISTORY LESSON

Ever since it was created, rum has tended to be on the side of the rebels. This was particularly true in the seventeenth century with its pirates and buccaneers, the time of the American Revolution, and more recent periods of unrest. There are three things at the origins of the spirit that we know today: the *pot still*, slaves and bloodily ruthless competition. The term 'globalisation' was introduced by rum (and sugar) to a waiting world, signifying the connections between Europe, America, Africa and the Caribbean through a complex trading web. And yet it all started quite simply with a plant, a grass actually.

Saccharum officinarum, better known as sugar cane, was grown in New Guinea about 10,000 years ago. By 6,000 BCE, sugar cane was being grown in Indonesia, the Philippines and India. At the time it was not used for distilling rum, although it was being used for the production of sugar and fermented drinks by 350 BCE. During one of his missions a certain man named Nearchus, one of Alexander the Great's generals, discovered 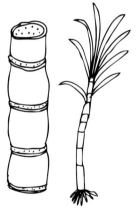 that a tribe in India used sugar cane to prepare sweet drinks. This discovery made sugar cane increasingly well-known and by the seventh century CE, the Arabs had laid their hands on sugar cane. The use of sugar cane became more widespread as the Arabs expanded their empire towards Cyprus, Malta and Sicily, the North African coast and from there to Spain and Portugal. At the time, sugar was an expensive product that was mainly used as a medicine. It symbolised wealth and richness, and sugar production became very important by the fifteenth century. That was when the Portuguese and Spanish began establishing colonies on the Canary Islands, Madeira and São Tomé. Those islands produced the bulk of European sugar by the first half of the fifteenth century; it was then transported to Antwerp and London to be refined. The Dutch and the English struggled for control of the lucrative sugar trade, but the Portuguese and the Spaniards had bigger plans for the sweet commodity. Before them lay an ocean that stretched to the riches in the Far East, or at least that was what Christopher Columbus thought...

CRAZY SUGAR CANE JUICE FOR THE SLAVES

During his second journey to America, Columbus decided to take some sugar cane cuttings to Hispaniola, an island in the Caribbean that is now shared by Haiti and the Dominican Republic. Hispaniola was followed by other islands such as Puerto Rico, Jamaica and Cuba and – although Columbus' main goal was to mine gold – sugar cane was planted everywhere. Portuguese explorers soon did the same in Brazil. There's nothing that grows better in a tropical climate than

sugar cane and no-one could work the plantations better than the indigenous populations. In 1516, the first primitive sugar factories were built on Hispaniola, and then in Brazil, Jamaica, Cuba and Puerto Rico. The Portuguese utilised the experience they had acquired in Africa during their attempts to evangelise the continent and began using African slaves on their Brazilian plantations. The logic of the Portuguese was that workers brought in from other continents were less likely to want to escape. Spain, England and France soon followed the example of the Portuguese and purchased slaves on a large scale to work on their sugar plantations. The door to modern slavery stood wide open from that moment on. Since it was believed that black people had lost their souls and lived in sin, immorality became commonplace.

By the end of the sixteenth century Jamaica, Cuba and Puerto Rico had huge sugar plantations and the slave trade was as profitable as the sugar trade. Despite this degrading history, African slaves played a significant role in the development of rum. The first reference to a distillate based on sugar cane can be found in a report from the governor of Bahia, Tomé de Sousa. It states that the slaves were appeased by *crazy sugar cane juice* or *cachaço* (now known as cachaça). This drink, made of unprocessed sugar cane juice, soon became popular among the slaves because it was easy to obtain and produce. And although cachaça is essentially a rum, modern interpretation defines rum as a by-product of sugar cane processing, i.e. based on molasses (see below).

RUM FOR THE FIRST TIME

The insatiable European urge for sugar soon resulted in the establishment of hundreds of sugar plantations in English, Spanish, French, Portuguese and Dutch colonies. By the middle of the seventeenth century, the British in Barbados and the French in Martinique had developed a system of plantations that turned the Caribbean into one large sugar factory and rum distillery. In 1655, Barbados was the largest sugar producer, with an annual yield of five million dollars.

However, the sugar cane plantations were facing a problem: what should they do with the waste? To make sugar, the harvested sugar cane has to be crushed to extract the juice. That juice is then boiled until it is reduced to crystallised sugar. The remaining unused juice or *molasses* was an inconvenient by-product in the seventeenth century: too bulky to be shipped, and nobody knew what to do with the molasses anyway. It was tried as cattle feed and as a medicine against syphilis, but in fact it was mostly just thrown away until some clever slave mixed the molasses with a bit of water and left it in the direct sunlight. The result? A seriously delicious drink! And as the art of distillation was making its way to the tropics at around that time, we can assume that rum must have been distilled for the first time around 1650.

BARBADOS,
OR MAYBE NOT...

It is highly likely that rum, both the spirit and the name, first came from Barbados. According to some historians, it was a Dutch emigrant named Peter Blower, who introduced the technique of distillation to the island in 1637. The first literary reference to rum dates back to 1651, when an anonymous author wrote, "The chief fuddling they make on the island is Rumbullion, alias Kill-Devil, and is made of sugar canes distilled, a hot, hellish, and terrible liquor." But let us first return to that 'highly likely' statement. In the same period, a similar incident took place on the French island of Martinique. Another Dutchman, named Benjamin Da Costa, taught the islanders there about distilling. Some even claim that rum was first made in Brazil.

However, as stated above, sugar cane distillates had already been brewed a century before the arrival of Peter and Benjamin: *aguardente de cana* (1533) or *cachaça* (1552). These distillates were very strong, had an unpleasant smell and tasted bitter. These precursors of rum were therefore primarily brewed to make money: they were definitely not fine quality spirits. And because those cane distillates were, for a long time, seen as a drink for slaves, it was quite a while before 'rum' was being mentioned in the printed word. And it spread from there.

RHUM

In 1751, the adventurous spirit was listed for the first time in the *Encyclopédie ou dictionnaire raisonné des sciences, des arts et des métiers*. In this seventeen-volume encyclopaedia, published by Diderot and Alembert, the authors referred to a spirit called *rhum*. The French were therefore the first to put the term *rhum* in print, although the exact origin of the word was still debatable at the time (see also 'What is rum?'). However, one thing is certain: for a long time rum was considered the lifeblood of the poor and corrupt; in that period, brandy and madeira were the spirits for the more sophisticated classes.

For this reason the first rum distillers were inexperienced and started working with stills that they did not really know how to use. They muddled along, mostly distilling for the money. It is not really clear when the turning point was, but thirst for money was probably the driving force then too. People became more and more aware that a better quality of rum meant more money. In the course of the eighteenth century, the English market really developed a taste for good rum. Whereas barely 800 litres were imported in 1698, that figure increased to about 8 million litres a hundred years later. Rum was no longer "hot and hellish", but rather fashionable.

AHOY MATEY!

Rum and pirates are inextricably intertwined. Everyone knows the *Pirates of the Caribbean* movies, in which Johnny Depp plays a pirate with a penchant for rum. "Why is the rum gone?" is still a popular quote from *The Curse of the Black Pearl*. But where does that association come from?

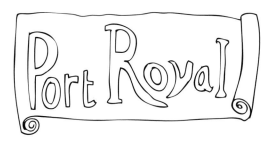

Well, in 1655 the British Royal Navy sailed to Jamaica to conquer the island, which they succeeded in doing reasonably easily. To defend the island, its inhabitants started building a fortress, which was called *Fort Cromwell* after their patron. A small community, *Point Cagway*, or in short, *The Point*, arose around the fortress, consisting largely of seamen, merchants, manual labourers and prostitutes. Not much later, the name of the village was changed to *Port Royal* and the first pirates were attracted by that royal name. Many of them had learned how to sail in their national navies, and at sea they also learned to drink rum. The crew of the British Royal Navy were also introduced to the domestic rum, and the daily ration of French brandy was replaced more and more frequently with Jamaican rum.

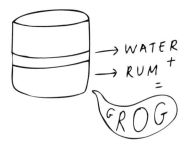

Officially, the British Royal Navy gave a ration of rum to its seamen twice a day from 1655 to 1970. Initially, this was pure necessity to counteract the dangers of boredom, mutiny and disease. But the pirates and the other seamen did not merely drink rum to have a good time. To provide the crew with sufficient fluid during long journeys, three liquids were taken on board: water, beer and rum. Since the water went rancid very quickly, it was drunk first, after which they switched to beer, and finally began drinking the rum. Strongly alcoholic, it has the longest shelf life.

Distributing an additional ration of rum was also a way of keeping the crew under control. Initially, the rum was given neat, or with lime juice, but this often left a lot of seamen too drunk to carry out their work properly, so water was later added to the rum. Admiral Edward Vernon introduced this custom in 1740... and grog was born! The following simple trick was used to make sure that the correct amount of water was added to the rum: a small amount of gunpowder was added to a glass of rum and the emulsion was heated using a magnifying glass between the glass and the sun until the gunpowder reached its ignition temperature. If the rum caught fire too, it was an indication that the drink contained too much alcohol. The rum therefore had to be diluted with water until only the gunpowder caught fire and not

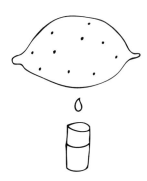

the rum itself. This custom was officially adopted by the Royal Navy and was used for more than two centuries. After it became known that scurvy is caused by a lack of vitamin C, lemon juice was added to the recipe.

THE VERY LAST BARREL: BLACK TOT DAY

By 1970, the daily distribution of rum rations (*tots*) to seamen had become no more than a dangerous tradition that had no place at all in modern times. However, navy personnel were still very sorry when the last portion of rum was poured on 31 July 1970. The day was christened *Black Tot Day* and seamen organised fake funerals and wore black mourning bands on all ships on duty worldwide. The frigate HMS Five was the last ship to throw a full barrel of rum overboard. That presumably did little for the mood on board, but it was clearly a safety precaution.

A VICIOUS RUM TRIANGLE

We will step back into the past for a while and focus on the time between the first and the last tots.
A really fascinating period! As rum became popular
with the navy, a flourishing export trade arose at the
end of the seventeenth century. The British colonies
shipped rum to Britain, where it was used in all kinds
of punches. Rum soon displaced gin and became
the most popular spirit. The New England region of
North America was also supplied abundantly with
rum. But because the British parliament had prohib-
ited the trade of distilled drinks between the colonies, exports of distilled rum were gradually replaced
by exports of molasses. And the ban naturally meant
that smuggling flourished. Shipping molasses to New
England was the foundation of the infamous trading
triangle involving rum and slavery.

In the eighteenth century, no fewer than four million slaves were purchased by the sugar-growing colonies. Most of them were intended for Brazil and the
British and French colonies. What did they buy slaves
with? Rum. A triangular
trade was set up between
Europe, America and Af-
rica. Ships from West-
ern Europe laden with
all kinds of merchan-
dise such as iron, weap-
ons and textiles left for
West Africa, where the
goods were exchanged
for slaves. Ships full of
slaves then sailed to the
Caribbean, where they
were sold as plantation
workers in exchange for

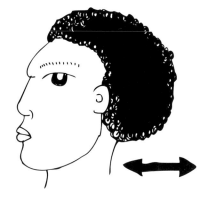

rum, sugar and other products such as coffee, cotton and tobacco.

The North American colonies simply loved rum, to put it mildly: vast amounts of sugar were transported to New England every day and used for distilling rum. The first rum distillers appeared in Boston, Massachusetts, in 1657. Distilling rum became a profitable industry in New England and the British colony soon became adept at producing the popular spirit. Rhode Island rum was worth as much as gold. The exchanges of slaves, molasses and rum flourished until the Sugar Act in 1764.

SUGAR ACT

The Sugar Act was a piece of fiscal legislation that was approved by the British parliament on 5 April 1764. The preamble to the act stated that setting up new regulations to improve the revenues of the kingdom was a priority, in particular to cover the costs of defending and protecting the empire and its many colonies. Another law had preceded the Sugar Act, namely the Molasses Act, which imposed a tax of sixpence a gallon on sugar syrup. However, that tax did not really get off the ground because of tax evasion by the colonies. It was then decided to halve the tax in conjunction with measures to impose the act more effectively on the inhabitants of the colonies; the British hoped that these measures would ensure payment of taxes.

However, the colonists were uncertain of the intentions of the British parliament; those worries were a root cause of the growing opposition movement that finally led to the American Revolution. The ports of New England in particular were hit hard by the Sugar Act, as the tougher enforcement of the act made smuggling sugar syrup much more dangerous. They therefore felt that the profits that could be made on rum were too small to justify a tax on sugar syrup. By the mid-eighteenth century it seemed that the end was nigh for the British and French sugar hegemony.

END OF THE SLAVE TRADE

It took until the eighteenth century before people throughout the world gradually turned their backs on human trafficking, with the rich naturally remaining staunch supporters of these ugly practices. However, it is not true that captive slaves always accepted their fate without a fight, even in the days when the trade was flourishing. There are numerous reports of slave rebellions. One of the first slave rebellions took place in 1683 in Barbados, while slaves in Jamaica regularly revolted too. Ultimately, however, those rebellions did not have a lasting effect. To put an end to slavery, the slaves' struggles had to be championed by other classes in the seat of imperialism. They found that support in William Wilberforce (1759-1833), a member of the British parliament, who campaigned for the abolition of the slave trade.

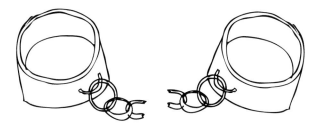

With the blessing of prime minister William Pitt the Younger (1759-1806) the first steps were taken towards putting an end to human trafficking. Pitt's position was that the slave trade had to be abolished because he believed it was more costly than hiring ordinary workers, basing his arguments on the theories of the free market economist Adam Smith. However, Pitt favoured the other camp when France abolished slavery in Saint-Domingue in 1794. In response Pitt sent troops to quash the slave army led by the French general Toussaint Louverture (1743-1803). But the British failed and left the island in 1798. Toussaint now held power in Hispaniola, however, he had not counted on Napoleon (1769-1821), who re-established slavery there in 1801. As a result, a new uprising broke out in Saint-Domingue. Meanwhile, the French troops were also combating a raging epidemic of yellow fever, and they were finally beaten at Vertières in 1803 by the troops of Toussaint's lieutenant, Jean-Jacques Dessalines (1760-1806). In 1804, Dessalines founded the republic of Haiti, only the second independent republic in the Western Hemisphere.

The independence of Haiti marked the beginning of the abolition of the slave trade. Great Britain finally abolished slavery in 1833 and ultimately France in 1848, which led to a drop in the production of sugar and rum. From then on sugar was imported from India and Java. Napoleon ordered studies on how sugar

could be extracted from sugar beets. In other words, the world started looking for sugar, molasses and rum from other sources. Cuba and Puerto Rico stepped forward.

CUBAN RUM

Europe was quietly turning its back on the sugar islands in the Caribbean. However, people in America were starting to get seriously addicted to sugar, and Cuba and Puerto Rico managed to feed that craving. Meanwhile, Jamaica became aware that higher profits could be generated from rum exports than from sugar production. Rum traders started creating their own brands and the increased rum production heralded an experimental era in terms of styles and flavours.

While previously the production of rum had been based on intuition, a new world was opened by the invention of the 'continuous still' and numerous new spirits were created. This distillation method not only yielded larger quantities, but also a paler rum. The continuous still first appeared in Europe, but Cuba in particular was delighted with the new distillation technique. As the island was still producing low grade rum and focusing largely on sugar exports, Aeneas Coffey's invention was a godsend. It let Cubans produce a high-quality rum, lighter and better than the familiar, dark Jamaican rum.

One of the most important people who helped refine Cuban rum was a Spaniard named Don Facundo Bacardí y Maso (1814-1886), who had settled in Cuba in 1834. The name undoubtedly rings a bell... Don Facundo experimented with filtering processes, distillation techniques and special types of yeast, managing to develop a softer, paler rum. On 4 February 1862 he founded the Bacardi y Compañía in Santiago de Cuba; just a small shop with a distillery.

Fun fact: Bats lived under the roof ridge of that building and it is more than likely that they were the inspiration for the world-famous logo. Other Cuban brands soon followed Bacardi's example. Matusalem, Camps and Havana Club were born.

RUM-RUNNERS DURING PROHIBITION

Alcohol consumption began to increase dramatically after the American War of Independence. In 1830, the average American drank almost two bottles of liquor a week, with the inevitable consequences. However, it took almost a century before the American Congress approved the Volstead Act that focused primarily on restricting alcohol consumption, although it also stated that alcohol could be used for other specific purposes. The rum distilleries could continue producing in America, because rum was needed to aromatise tobacco.

However, alcohol was no longer easily available and a whole generation of Americans entered the criminal milieu. The leading figure was without a doubt Al Capone. Alcohol could still be bought in Mexico, Canada and the Caribbean, and a lot of people started smuggling liquor: they were called rum-runners. The liquor ban also marked the beginning of the Bacardi phenomenon and the beginning of the golden age of rum cocktails.

BACARDI AND COKE

The Great Depression – the economic crisis in America during the nineteen thirties – caused a downward spiral in sugar production in the Caribbean. Many distilleries had to close and by 1938 the number in Jamaica dropped from one hundred to only twenty-nine. Rum was displaced by whisky and gin; rum only became more popular again with the advent of the Second World War when rum was as indispensable to the British soldiers as food; they had to muster up their courage before they went into battle.

Immediately after the war, rum was neglected again. Consumer tastes changed drastically and lighter, vodka-based cocktails became fashionable. But trends are volatile, as we all know, and Bacardi managed to revive the rum landscape. This heralded the era of the big rum brands. Everyone had names such as Captain Morgan and Lamb's Navy Rum on their lips.

By 1960, consumers were no longer looking just for their favourite style of rum, they preferred specific big brands. Young people in particular greatly preferred the lighter spirits. Bacardi was no longer a kind of rum, it was just Bacardi. Bacardi and Coke – everyone's tried one!

People may even ask specifically for that (rather than for the generic mixer or a Cuba Libre), although it's no more than rum and cola, no more special than a gin and tonic. Point taken? The emergence of exotic tiki cocktails after the Second World War also helped rum to become popular again.

RUM TODAY

Since the second half of the twentieth century, rum has become increasingly popular, driven by tourism in particular. A lot of Americans and Europeans holidaying in rum-producing countries fell for the local spirit. Yet in those days people mainly drank rum mixed with Coca-Cola or in all kinds of cocktails. Today this has changed: more and more consumers want their rum neat.

Why has rum suddenly become attractive again now? For the same reason rum was pushed aside: it is a spirit without rules. Whereas whisky and bourbon are

bound by strict regulations regarding ingredients, maturation and production, rum is less dependent on rules, which allows the producers to freewheel. The current generation is flirting with this freedom, letting it discover and explore spirits that blur the boundaries.

However, this has also created a lot of misunderstandings about what good rum is. Let's put it even more bluntly: there's a good chance that most consumers have never drunk a good rum. We would love to change that, of course! There are a lot of premium brands in the

market with a long and glorious history, a rich past that you can taste in your glass. Drinks made of sugar cane juice, the basic ingredient of rum, are among the oldest alcoholic products in the world, and awareness of this is what makes rum so attractive today. We are living in an age when authentic products are hot, and rum very definitely falls into that category. Rum, like tequila, has a broad spectrum of flavours and colours, from clear to brown, light to heavy, spicy to floral. There is something for everyone! Every reason to go on an adventure.

Trendsetting bartenders and mixologists are more and more likely to use premium rum in classic cocktails such as the Manhattan or the Old Fashioned, because rum has a more neutral background yet it is complex enough to take the cocktail to the next level.

Besides the fact that rum is increasingly getting the recognition that it deserves and renewed attention from the world of mixology, there are also some other developments that have helped rum to be taken seriously again. Organisations such as ACR (Authentic Caribbean Rum) are trying to ensure that rules are imposed on rum production. A certain number of rules and legislations will undoubtedly help guarantee the quality of rum. And like whisky and bourbon, traditional distilleries are now focusing their attention on rum and breathing new life into the rum landscape.

A lot of changes are also underway in the scientific field. Bryan Davis of Lost Spirit Distillery, for instance, is said to have invented a chemical reactor that makes it possible to give spirits the character of a twenty-year period of maturation in just six days. The reactor is currently still in the test phase, but if it delivers on its promise it will undoubtedly trigger a small revolution in the drinks landscape. Bryan hopes to reinvigorate forgotten spirits: rather than expensive maturation taking many years, the process might now only take six days. But even more importantly, this reactor will suddenly set the bar much higher for low-quality spirits. Just imagine that a mediocre rum can be given the character of one that has matured for twenty years in wooden barrels, all in a mere six days. This would also be a blessing for small distilleries that cannot afford to leave their products maturing for lengthy periods. Finally, this reactor will undoubtedly encourage the distillers' creativity. Rather than having to wait twenty years before you know whether a recipe is successful or not, you could already get answers after just six days. This opens up a world of possibilities! By the end of 2014, Lost Spirits Distillery had a product on the market that had undergone maturation in the reactor: *Lost Spirits Colonial American Inspired Rum*. Despite this rum's ponderous name, it turned out to be a real hit. If Davis' invention delivers on its promise, we are at the dawn of a completely new world.

PRODUCTION PROCESS

THE SWEET GRASS...

There's no rum without sugar cane. So it's important for us to take a moment to consider this sweet grass. Sugar cane or *Saccharum officinarum* belongs to the family of grasses that originates from Papua New Guinea, where people chewed the stalks and drank the sweet juice.

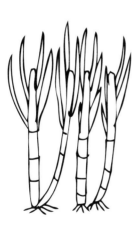

However, the first sugar cane plantations were set up in India: the sugar cane was taken from Indonesia to India, and people started to grow sugar cane around 500 BCE. The sugar cane juice was thickened until it became a solid that could be kept for a long time. Nearchos, one of the generals of Alexander the Great, was introduced to sugar around 300 BCE in India. He described it as "a cane that produces honey without bees".

During the Middle Ages, the Arabs introduced the knowledge of cultivating sugar cane and producing sugar to the Mediterranean. In the fifteenth century, the Spanish and the Portuguese also started growing sugar cane in their colonies on the Canary Islands and Madeira. From there, sugar spread to the Caribbean

and Brazil. From then on, sugar became the most important product of a triangular trading pattern (see also 'A brief history lesson') between the New World, Europe and Africa.

Sugar is still important today for the economies of Barbados, the Dominican Republic, Guadeloupe, Jamaica, Grenada and other islands in the Caribbean. The sweet grass is grown in more than 100 countries with tropical or subtropical climates. The largest producers are Brazil, India and China. Sugar cane is also currently being used for biofuel, which is another factor driving up production in South America.

PLANTING AND HARVESTING SUGAR CANE

As mentioned earlier, sugar cane feels most at home in tropical and subtropical climates.

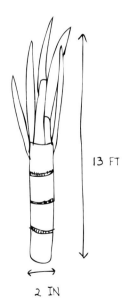

The cane can grow up to 3 or 4 metres (10-13 ft) in height, and the stalk can be as much as 5 centimetres (2 inch) thick. The plant can be grown three months each year on most plantations without needing irrigation systems. Plantations with irrigation systems can harvest all year round. The sugar cane cuttings may be planted manually or mechanically. Propagation takes place by taking stem cuttings that are then planted. Multiple shoots can be harvested from a single plant cutting. The leaves of the plant are burned away just before harvesting so that the canes, which contain the sugar, can be cut more easily. Burning off the fields is still standard

13 FT

2 IN

practice in South Africa and Mauritius, but it is no longer allowed in Brazil.

During harvesting, the plant is cut off just above the ground. This is still done manually in some areas (mainly locations that cannot be reached by mechanical harvesters, such as steep slopes), but mechanical harvesting is increasingly common. The stalks are then processed to extract the juice. The extract from the first pressing is called 'virgin honey'. The sugar is then crystallised, after which the molasses remain.

The sugar cane juice, the virgin honey and the molasses can all be used for making rum. The remaining stalk residues, also known as *bagasse*, are used as raw material for paper, as cattle fodder or as fuel.

PROCESSING SUGAR CANE: FROM PURE SUGAR CANE JUICE TO VIRGIN HONEY TO MOLASSES

Since no production methods have been prescribed for rum, its production is based on traditional processing methods that vary depending on the location and the distillery.

No matter whether you use sugar cane juice, virgin honey or molasses for making rum, the juice has to be extracted from the canes first. When the canes leave the field, they are 10%-13.5% sugar by weight. The canes are washed and dust and dirt are removed.

After that, they are chopped into pieces mechanically and the fibres are removed. Preparing the canes is very important, as the amount of sugar that can be extracted later on depends on this stage. The canes are then crushed under large, heavy wheels in a grinding mill. Water is added during this process to dilute the juice and to allow a second pressing if necessary. The juice is filtered after that and clarified until pure sugar cane juice remains. At this stage, the sugar cane juice contains about 16% sugar.

To raise the sugar concentration to 60% by total weight, the filtrate is heated to make sure that the excess water evaporates. The result of this evaporation is the virgin honey. The virgin honey is then boiled until sugar crystals begin to form. The sugar crystals are extracted from the thick syrup by centrifuging. They are dried and the remaining brown liquid is boiled for the second or third time to leave dark, sticky molasses. The dark mass of molasses still consists of about 55% uncrystallised sugar, as well as a lot of minerals and other components that determine the aroma and flavour of the rum later.

FERMENTATION

Fermentation occurs after yeast is added to the molasses or the sugar cane juice (mainly in the French Antilles). This converts sugar that is still present into

carbon dioxide and ethanol. Pure molasses are not fermented: water is first added to give a mixture with a sugar content of approximately 15%.

The rum industry is not bound by specific laws and regulations, so both natural and controlled fermentation techniques can therefore be used. One of the most recent trends in fermentation is continuous fermentation using a column configuration.

NATURAL FERMENTATION

The natural fermentation process is very similar to brewing beer. Distilleries use natural yeasts from the air and in the sugar cane juice that can convert sugars into alcohol. This fermentation method takes place in open containers to maximise exposure of the liquid to the air, and takes about one to two weeks, depending on the size of the container. It is an impressive process to see. If you have the opportunity to visit a distillery that uses natural fermentation, you certainly should. It seems as if the liquid in the tank is dancing to an imaginary beat as it bubbles away. The result of natural fermentation is unpredictable, often ending with something that isn't quite what was wanted.

CONTROLLED FERMENTATION

Specific yeast strains are used for controlled fermentation and the exact type of yeast often depends on the distillery. In other words, a distillery's distinctive nature can depend on cultivating its own yeast strain, which can create the typical flavour of a certain rum and that yeast is often a carefully kept secret. To prevent the liquid from fermenting naturally, small amounts of the batch are repeatedly tested by adding yeast in a controlled way. The yeast can then do its work. More juice is added gradually until a large quantity of concentrated liquid has been created. This is finally put in large fermentation tanks. Controlled fermentation usually takes only two to three days and the results are very predictable.

CONTINUOUS OR COLUMN FERMENTERS

Fermenting sugar cane juice or molasses in a column configuration is a recent technique. As the name suggests, this method uses a main tank that is continuously provided with diluted molasses. The flow of molasses keeps the yeast alive. At the same time as the incoming flow, an equal amount of liquid is extracted elsewhere from the fermentation tank. That liquid – *the wash* – is ready to be distilled.

DISTILLATION

Distillation is probably the most essential step in making rum. The main objective of distillation is to separate the alcohol from the fermented wash. The secondary objective of distillation is to remove impurities from the alcohol. After fermentation, the wash has an alcohol content of 6%-8.5%. Distillation will give a much higher alcohol content and eliminate substances from the liquid by evaporation. Two methods are used

for distilling rum: the *pot still* (batch distillation) and the *continuous still* (column distillation).

POT-STILLED RUM

Pot stilling is the most traditional distillation technique and is also known as 'batch distillation'. Because the amount of liquid that can be put into the boiler (kettle) is limited, the fluid has to be distilled in batches. This technique is very labour-intensive, because the kettle has to be cleaned between the various batches. The residues after distillation are known as *dunder*. This can be processed and used as biofuel or cattle feed. But some distillers collect the dunder in *dunder pits*. These notorious pits are not always exactly a model of hygiene. The stench coming from them is awful and many animals that come near the pits faint and fall in. Dunder is often added to the fermenting molasses to give more character to the final distillate. This does not pose any danger to health because the rum is distilled several times. The technique is regularly used in Jamaica in particular. But let's return to pot-stilled rum...

A pot still consists of three parts: the distillation kettle in which the liquid is boiled, the condenser that cools the vapour down and the gooseneck that takes the vapour to the condenser. The first distillate, also known as a 'single distillate', still contains a lot of impurities and is almost always distilled a second time. Some distilleries go even further and distil three or even four times to obtain a crystal-clear result. A pot-stilled rum usually has a deeper and more intense flavour, but it is not as pure as a continuously distilled rum.

CONTINUOUSLY DISTILLED RUM

The switch from kettle distillation to distillation columns was made for the first time during the Industrial Revolution, when a certain Aeneas Coffey of Dublin perfected an earlier invention by Robert Stein. The idea behind this columnar configuration, the continuous still, is as simple as it is brilliant: Instead of having the distillation process take place in various boilers, Coffey built a layout of interconnected kettles in which the liquid is distilled continuously.

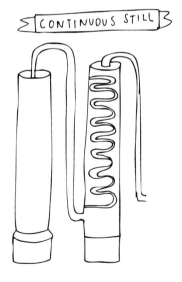

CONTINUOUS STILL

A column still consists of a number of permeable modules that allow alcohol-rich gas to rise through perforated plates on the one hand, while the liquid and heavier constituents trickle back down through drains on the other. The higher the gases go, the lighter they are and the more concentrated the alcohol will be. The point at which the gases are drawn off determines the purity of the alcohol. This will usually be between 80%-96%.

The system was initially designed to make the distillation process more consistent and less labour-intensive. Rum that is distilled using this method can be crystal clear, but sometimes lacks the traditional flavour often associated with rum.

MATURATION PROCESS

No other spirit manages to squeeze so many colours, aromas and flavours into a single bottle as rum. It ranges from a clear, colourless spirit to a universe of gold and brown shades, or even almost black. Rum can range from a transparent adolescent into a seasoned bon vivant. This is mainly the result of maturation, but can also come from adding caramel and other colorants, filtration or the magic in the bottle. This chapter discusses the maturation process of rum in more detail. Ageing definitely plays a role in rum.

THE BARRELS

Most distillers mature their rum in oak barrels that have previous been used for whisky or bourbon. Bourbon always has to be matured in new barrels, which is why there is always a surplus of used barrels available. These are sold off cheaply, for instance to the rum sector. Most barrels come from the United States and Canada, although some – admittedly to a lesser extent – come from Europe, where they are used for maturing Scotch, cognac or sherry. French limousin barrels are used in rare cases, mainly for *rhum agricole* (see also 'Classification').

The inside of a new barrel is usually charred first before it is used for maturing spirits. The charred inside of the barrels is removed first by some distillers when the cask is used for a second time. Others repeat the charring on the inside, or simply refill the barrel without changing anything. The chemistry of maturation

has still not been fully explored, but it is generally reckoned that the maturation process improves and softens a fresh distillate. While the rum is dormant in the barrels, the natural tannins in the wood create a golden glow that develops after a number of years into a deep brown colour. The alcohol in rum acts as a solvent, leaching the tannins from the wood. In addition to changing the colour, the tannins also give a mild vanilla flavour and a delicate oaky touch. The possibilities for maturing rum are extremely diverse, bearing witness to the creativity of the distillers and the intended goal. Barrels previously used for port, sherry and madeira create delicate overtones of raisins and dried fruit and even add extra tannins to the rum. Rum that is laid down in single malt barrels gets a touch of the single malt whisky. Sometimes, rum is matured in two different barrels, for instance first in oak and then in madeira barrels to give it an extra finish.

ALCOHOL PERCENTAGE

Most rum producers mature rum at an alcohol content of 70%-80%, but some distillers prefer to mature their rum at an alcohol content that is closer to the final alcohol content in the bottle, namely 40%-45%. A lower alcohol content leaches somewhat lighter esters and phenols from the barrels, whereas a higher alcohol content draws out heavier compounds and flavours. Most distilleries prefer a higher alcohol content because this requires fewer barrels. On the other hand, a stronger rum evaporates more quickly, which results in greater losses. This evaporation loss is also known as the *angels' share*, as if referring to angels who come to collect their tithe of the spirit.

THE ANGELS' SHARE...

Most rum is matured in the country of origin. Of course, maturation in tropical countries gives a totally different result to maturation in Scotland, for instance. Warmer temperatures will make alcohol evaporate more quickly. This evaporation is also known as the *angels' share*. Whereas in Scotland only 2% of the alcohol evaporates per year while laid down, this can run up to 10% in the tropics. In other words, the angels in the Caribbean can hold boozier parties than their companions in Scotland!

In any event, the more alcohol that evaporates, the more air there will be in the barrel. That is why some producers apply *ouillage*, a term that comes from the wine sector. It refers to regularly topping up barrels. As the rum barrels are topped up every year with rum from the same year, maturation takes places more gradually, and the rum will not be subject to undesirable changes in flavour.

CARAMEL

Before the rum is finally bottled, water is first added to ensure the right alcohol content. This water not only dilutes the rum, but also affects its colour. Caramel is therefore often added to give the matured rum its tempting colour back. In addition, not all barrels will give the same colour, which is why caramel is added to obtain a consistent colour. Black rums are often the result of excess caramel being added.

BLENDING

Rum is often blended after maturing to ensure a consistent final result. But it may be the case that a particular barrel of rum tastes so exceptional that the distillery decides to bottle it and market it as a limited edition *single cask or single barrel* rum. Rums of different ages and from different barrels are mixed during blending. The flavour of any given barrel is affected not only by the number of years of maturation, but also by where it was kept. Samples from different barrels are therefore taken and tasted, and the rums from the selected barrels are finally mixed until the flavour matches the flavour profile that the master distiller had in mind. In exceptional cases, the blend may be matured a second time. This second maturation will also ensure subtle flavour nuances.

THE SOLERA SYSTEM

The solera system is a labour-intensive way of maturing rum. It is often used for Spanish-style rums. It results in a quicker maturation process and a constant rum quality. However, some consider this system to be cheating, as the rum producers often state the age of the oldest rum on the bottle label, whereas the average age of the rums used is actually much lower.

So how does the solera system work? The system can be shown as an inverted pyramid, in which barrels of the same rum but of different ages are stacked. The oldest rum is always at the bottom and the youngest at the top. When a proportion of the rum at the bottom (i.e. the oldest) is bottled, that barrel is topped up with rum from a barrel above it, which in turn is supplemented with even younger rums. When the barrel at the top is finally empty, it is filled with fresh rum and the process starts all over again.

There is nothing wrong with the system and it often yields surprising results. But – as is quite often the case with rum – not all producers are equally honest in terms of the information they provide on the bottle label.

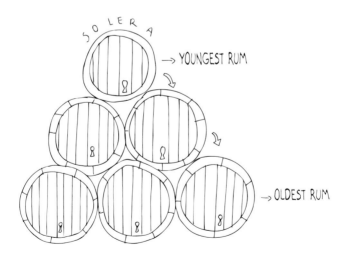

CLASSIFICATION

Classifying rum is not as easy as it seems. It is one of the most diverse spirits in the world and there is little or no legislation covering its production. The flavour and aroma are often location-specific and depend on the terroir, local distillation methods and local traditions. Nevertheless, in this chapter we will try to classify all the various kinds and styles of rum.

We will focus on 'rhum agricole' and 'traditional rum' first. After that, we will take a look at the colour of the various kinds of rum and finish by arranging our spirits into the English, French and Spanish styles. These different styles also include rums that are given a separate classification, e.g. *aged rums*, *blends*, *flavoured rums* and *spiced rums*. Of course, rum would not be rum if it didn't live up to its rebellious reputation. We therefore had to create a separate classification for the 'outsiders' that do not fit under any one heading.

RHUM AGRICOLE AND TRADITIONAL RUM, OR RHUM VERSUS RUM

In fact, rums can be split into two basic groups: rhum agricole and traditional rum, which is also known as industrial rum. Rhum agricole is rum that is produced using freshly pressed sugar cane juice, whereas traditional or industrial rum is made using molasses. Furthermore, rhum agricole is a French-style rum, whereas traditional and industrial rum are more in line with the Spanish and English styles.

Note!

The contradiction in the terms 'traditional' and 'industrial' rum is striking. Traditional and industrial are words that do not normally belong together. It is very likely that this derives from French chauvinism: rums that were not rhum agricole, were immediately deemed to be 'industrial'. Of course, this resulted in a counter-reaction from the Spanish and English, who considered their rum styles to be 'traditional'.

COLOUR GRADATIONS

CLEAR RUM/WHITE RUM

Light rum, also known as 'white', 'silver', 'clear', 'crystal' or 'blanc' rum, is usually a rum that was matured for less than a year. Only a few white rums mature longer: among these are the Caroni Superb White Magic, which has to be laid down for seven years. The matured white rums are passed through a charcoal filter, giving them the flavour of a dark rum but not the colour. Many people believe that white rum is only meant for use as a mixer, but a premium white rum can be drunk neat too.

BROWN RUM/GOLDEN RUM

Rums with a golden or amber colour are also called 'gold' or 'oro'. These rums have a medium body and get their colour either from the oak barrels they mature in or from added caramel.

DARK BROWN RUM

These rums are slightly darker than the previous category. They are usually dark brown, but they can also be red or black. They have matured in heavily charred barrels for a lengthy period, which is why they have a more pronounced flavour: more spicy, often with strong notes of caramel.

Note!
When looking for quality rum, the best thing to do is not to rely on the colour, since some cheap white rum brands colour their rum with caramel until it becomes dark brown. This is done to mislead unknowing consumers.

STYLES

ENGLISH STYLE

TRADITIONAL/INDUSTRIAL RUM

English style rums are often dark, with a full flavour and a rich aroma. English rum emphasises the molasses used. This is also the style of the rum with the longest history.

COUNTRIES
Jamaica, Barbados, Trinidad & Tobago, Virgin Islands, Antigua, St. Lucia, British Guyana (Demerara), Belize, Mauritius
BASIC PRODUCT
Molasses
PRODUCTION METHOD
Lengthy fermentation – pot still distillation – long maturation in oak barrels
FLAVOUR AND AROMA
Spicy, vivid, dark, heavy, strong

RHUM AGRICOLE

These rums are made from fresh sugar cane juice, and you can taste it. They retain the original flavour of sugar cane. They are elegant and often slightly more expensive than the rums that are produced using molasses. During maturation, the *ouillage* technique (see also 'Maturation process') is often used.

COUNTRIES
  Martinique, Guadeloupe, Marie-Galante, Haiti, Réunion, French Guyana
BASIC PRODUCT
  Pure sugar cane juice
PRODUCTION METHOD
  Column still (except for rhum agricole from Haiti)
FLAVOUR AND AROMA
  Fruity, intense, floral, earthy, complex, elegant

TRADITIONAL/INDUSTRIAL RUM

These are usually light rums with a clean flavour. They only conquered the rum market later on. Spanish style rums often use the solera system (see also 'Maturation process'). The age stated on the bottle is often the average of the rums used, not the age of the oldest rum.

COUNTRIES
  Cuba, Puerto Rico, Dominican Republic, Venezuela, Guatemala, Nicaragua, Panama, Colombia, Peru, Costa Rica, Ecuador
BASIC PRODUCT
  Molasses
PRODUCTION METHOD
  Short fermentation – column still
FLAVOUR AND AROMA
  Buttery, rounded, sweet

CLASSIFICATION WITHIN THE STYLES

Further classification of certain rums within the various styles is required. For instance, within the English, French and Spanish styles you can also find *aged rums*, *blends*, *flavoured rums* and *spiced rums*.

AGED

Aged simply means that the rum was matured, regardless of whether it was matured for a short or long period of time. There are no uniform laws or rules that determine how long a rum has to mature in order to be labelled as 'aged'. As stated earlier, white rums too are often laid down so that they can mature. It is therefore not true for rum that dark-coloured is synonymous with mature!

BLENDS

For the sake of clarity: almost all rums are blends, made from various barrels of different ages, with the exception of *single barrel* or *single cask* products. However, we use the term 'blend' to mean rums that incorporate various characteristics to obtain a single rum.

An example may make it a little clearer. Plantation Original Dark is a blend of rum from Jamaica and

Trinidad. Both countries produce English-style rums but still have their own characteristics, which you can find in Plantation Dark Original.

Most brands that put a blend on the market work with various distilleries from all over the world. They buy rums, both matured and young, and let them mature further in their own country to eventually create a perfect blend. Other brands have distilleries in various countries and use their own rums to create blends.

FLAVOURED RUMS

These rums are infused or flavoured with extracts that give the rum its typical flavour. These could be, for instance, mango, coconut, vanilla, lime or banana. The alcohol content of flavoured rums is usually below 40% and they are served neat or on the rocks.

Note!

Flavoured rum is actually the commercialised variant of the famous 'rhum arrangé', which is traditionally made in Guadeloupe, Madagascar and Réunion. 'Rhum arrangé' is rum in which tropical fruits and/or spices have been macerated. You may have seen the big glass jars at the back of the drinks cabinet in a bar in some tropical country and wondered what was in them.

SPICED RUMS

Herbs and sometimes caramel are added to spiced rums. They are mostly dark brown and based on a golden or brown rum. Herbs that are commonly used include vanilla, cinnamon, rosemary, pepper and aniseed. Sugar and honey are often used to sweeten these rums.

OUTSIDERS

The outsiders are rums that cannot be classified under a single heading. They are 'out of the box' or a combination of various styles. Independent bottlers, who select barrels of rum from various distilleries and let them mature further if necessary to create a rum of their own, are also considered outsiders.

NOT QUITE RUM...

CACHAÇA

Cachaça is a Brazilian spirit that could be classified as a rhum agricole as it is closely related to white rum and produced from freshly pressed sugar cane juice. The alcohol content of cachaça should be between

38%-54% and sugar may be added (up to 6 grams/litre). To obtain an 'aged cachaça', the producer must ensure that at least 50% of its spirit matures for at least one year. Sometimes caramel is added to give the cachaça a darker colour.

Cachaça is very much the national drink of Brazil and the main ingredient in a caipirinha (a common cocktail). The best-known cachaça brand in the Benelux countries is undoubtedly Pitu. Leblon, Ypioca, Abelha, Cachaça 51, Canario and Avua are other well-known brands of cachaça.

CLAIRIN

Clairin is an indigenous rum style from Haiti that resembles rhum agricole in many ways. This of course is due to the fact that Haiti was a French colony for a long time. Clairin is a well-crafted and straightforward type of rum that is rarely found outside Haiti. Just like rhum agricole, sugar cane juice is used as the basis rather than molasses. When producing clairin, the sugar cane juice is thickened over a fire of squeezed sugar cane stalks, known as *bagasse*. After that, the juice can be stored for eighteen months before it is distilled. This ensures that clairin can be produced the whole year round.

Natural yeast is used to ferment the juice. In other words: the juice is simply exposed to the air in large uncovered barrels in the hope that it will come into contact with natural yeasts. Luckily, yeast is pretty much omnipresent at locations where sugar cane is processed, and the sugar cane juice is ready for distillation after seven to ten days. Distillation is always done twice and clai-

rin is usually bottled without adding water. In other words, clairin is a strong spirit with an alcohol content that usually ranges between 50%-60%.

Clairin is not very well-known over here in Europe, at least not yet. There is only a single importer based in Italy who imports three types of clairin into Europe: Vava (Arawaks Distillery), Casimir (Douglas Casimir Distillery) and Sajou (Chelo Distillery).

The Gargano rum classification

A new form of classification has been making major strides since 2017. This form is based on the production methods, regardless of origin, style or colour.

The classification was thought up by Luca Gargano, the driving force behind the rum bottler Velier, together with Richard Seale, who is the man behind the Foursquare Distillery in Barbados.

The aim is to give the rum a system of labelling comparable to that of whiskies, so that it is clear to the consumer which are the higher quality products. A single malt whisky, for example, is generally thought superior (justifiably or otherwise) to a blended whisky...

The four labels that supporters of the Gargano classification system want to see on the bottles are:
- Pure single rum: rum that has been distilled in a pot still;
- Single blended rum: a blend of rums distilled in pot stills and traditional column stills;
- Traditional rum: rum distilled in a traditional column still;
- Modern rum: rum distilled in modern multi-column stills.

A distinction is also made according to the raw material used: sugar cane juice or molasses. Here is a diagram showing the basic idea.

	Sugar cane juice	Molasses
100% pot still	Pure single *rhum agricole*	Pure single rum
Blended pot still and traditional column still	-	Single blended rum
100% traditional column still	*Rhum agricole*	Traditional rum
100% industrial multi-column still	-	Modern rum

In our opinion, this classification very much deserves a place in the world of rum. Purists can see straight away from the labels what kind of rum they are buying. We do however fear that the larger brands will not adopt this classification, because they would all virtually end up in the "modern rum" category. Because of its industrial connotation, this category does not sound very appealing.

A "pure single rum" is still no guarantee of a good rum either. Both Velier and Foursquare market rums that are real jewels, but there are other producers that are less to our taste. Added to that is the question of whether the average consumer will prefer the taste of a "pure single rum" to a "single blended rum" or even a "modern rum"?

Furthermore, not all producers are keen to reveal the production methods they use. We nevertheless hope that the new Gargano classification will make things more transparent for the end consumers.

RUM
BRANDS

Unfortunately, rum is still not taken seriously enough, other than by bartenders and mixologists who have embraced rum for some time. All too often ordinary consumers still associate rum with hula dancing and poorly made daiquiris. Not to mention the coke that they pour over it. Admittedly, some rums do taste better if you pour coke over them, but a high-quality rum is generally not mixed with soft drinks. After all, you would never add a mixer to a single malt whisky. Luckily, uninformed rum drinkers are gradually making way for a totally new generation that treats the spirit with respect and looks for the real jewels, which they drink neat. This is because rum offers a wide range of flavours and plenty of choice if you want to go exploring. What makes rum even more attractive? A high-quality bottle will not cost you a fortune.

In this chapter we go looking for the best treasures among rums, focusing on the various styles and their flavours in even more detail. We will also give a quick explanation of the flavour star.

VARIOUS STYLES OF RUM

This book mainly deals with high-quality premium rums: mischievous, passionate and complex. Rum contains a full spectrum of flavours from dry to packed full of tropical fruits. Some are light and festive, others are dark and luscious. They are perfectly good on their own, but can also give exceptional depth to cocktails. That is exactly why it is not easy to pin down the wide spectrum of rum to any single flavour. Rum manages to surprise us over and over again and it is able to bring out totally different flavours each time we drink it.

In this chapter we have tried to give the most comprehensive overview possible of the premium rum brands. We have classified the brands by their various styles – English, French or Spanish – and each will be given a place in the flavour star. After that, each of the various bottles (types of rum) produced by the brand is subdivided further, where appropriate, into *aged*, *blend*, *flavoured* and *spiced*. This results in a useful guideline for choosing a bottle of rum. Just to remind you...

ENGLISH STYLE
TRADITIONAL/INDUSTRIAL RUM

English rums are heavier because the pot still distillation technique is often used. This is one of the oldest rum styles, resulting in aromatic structures and flavours with overtones of fruit and tobacco, for instance. These rums sacrifice purity slightly and are generally sweeter.

FRENCH STYLE
RHUM AGRICOLE

French rums are characterised by green and vegetal tones, because pure sugar cane juice is used. This creates the smell of fresh cut grass and the flavour of a fresh summer morning. In our opinion, French rum also has the *funkiest* flavour.

SPANISH STYLE
TRADITIONAL/INDUSTRIAL RUM

Spanish rums are light and pure. They are characterised by their dry flavour and buttery texture. The focus is on creating the softest spirit possible with sugar cane as the main flavour. Because molasses are used, it does not have the vegetal tone that is found in French rums.

HORS CATÉGORIE

Hors catégorie are the 'outsiders', rums that cannot be placed under any single heading. They are 'out of the box' or a combination of various styles.

Where possible, we go a step further for each brand and subdivide their various types into aged, blend, flavoured or spiced.

- AGED RUMS simply means that the rum was matured, regardless of whether this was done for a short or long period.
- We use the term BLEND to mean rums that incorporate various characteristics or styles to obtain a single rum.
- FLAVOURED RUMS are infused or flavoured with extracts that give the rum its typical flavour.
- SPICED RUMS have herbs added, and sometimes caramel too. They are mostly dark brown and based on a golden or brown rum.

It is impossible to list all bottles for every brand; some brands have as many as fifty or more types, and some of them are very hard to find. We have limited our list to the most popular and most easily available bottles.

FLAVOUR STAR 2.0 AND OUR FIFTY CHOSEN ONES

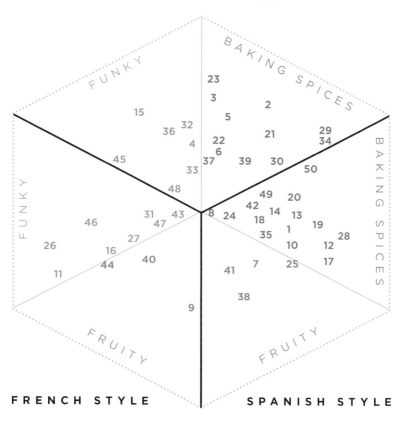

ENGLISH STYLE

FUNKY

BAKING SPICES

BAKING SPICES

FUNKY

FRUITY

FRUITY

FRENCH STYLE

SPANISH STYLE

23
3
15
2
36 32
5
4
21
22
29
6
34
45
37 39 30
50
33
48
49 20
42 14 13
31 43 8 24 18 19
46 47 35 1 28
27 10 12
26 16 7 25 17
44 40 41
11
38
9

OUR FIFTY SELECTIONS AND THEIR PLACE IN THE FLAVOUR STAR

As said earlier, it is almost impossible to pin rum down to any particular flavour. The range is too diverse and due to the lack of a general standard, producers can freewheel to their heart's content. Admittedly, rum is a rebel, but so are we! We have therefore selected fifty rums that we have placed at specific points in our flavour star.

We selected fifty rums on the basis of their quality and availability. In other words: all rums in the Flavour Star 2.0 are not only delicious but also readily available. We first classified our chosen rums by style, after which we gave them a specific place according to their dominant flavour.

The closer the rum gets to the centre of our flavour star, the simpler or 'cleaner' its flavour is: no frills, purity at its best. The further any given rum moves from the centre, the more complex its flavour is: a helter-skelter of flavour nuances. We then subdivided each style into two dominant flavours that overlap for each style. For instance, we subdivided the English style into the flavours *funky* and *baking spices*, the French style into *funky* and *fruity* and the Spanish style into *fruity* and *baking spices*.

FUNKY

Vegetal tones and funky features. What we mean by 'funky' is the slightly atypical aroma that probably scares a beginner, but is a real turn-on for an experienced rum lover. Think of a playful, almost undefinable musky scent.

FRUITY

Tropical fruit tones

BAKING SPICES

Spicy with flavours such as vanilla, caramel, butterscotch, cinnamon, cloves... Think of typical baking spices.

ENGLISH STYLE

English-style rums are often dark, with a full flavour and a rich aroma. English rum emphasises the molasses used. This is also the style of rum with the longest history.

COUNTRIES
Jamaica, Barbados, Trinidad & Tobago, Virgin Islands, Antigua, St. Lucia, British Guyana (Demerara), Belize, Mauritius

BASIC PRODUCT
Molasses

PRODUCTION METHOD
Long fermentation period – pot still distillation – long maturation period in oak barrels

FLAVOUR AND AROMA
Spicy, vivid, dark, heavy, strong

1931

ORIGIN

In February 1931, St. Lucia Distillers celebrated the inauguration of their newest distillery in Mabouya Valley, St. Lucia with this rum. The distillery was started by Denis Barnard and produced rum until Dennery and Roseau merged in 1972. The company acquired the name St. Lucia Distillers after the merger. You can find the history on the packaging and on every bottle. Every year a new edition is brought on the market and the colour of the label is changed. In addition, all bottles are numbered and are real collector's items for rum connoisseurs around the globe.

FLAVOUR AND AROMA

Bourbon barrels are used for maturation; port barrels are sometimes used too. Every edition is also a blend that stands on its own: sometimes column and kettle distillates are mixed, and sometimes only column distillates are used. The makers play with various combinations of used bourbon and port barrels for maturation too. For final maturation, the distillate is laid down in American oak.

Name	Alc. %	🏛	🌿	🍍	🛢
1931 ST LUCIA XO 1ˢᵗ edition	43				▾
1931 ST LUCIA XO 2ⁿᵈ edition	43				▾
1931 ST LUCIA XO 3ʳᵈ edition	43				▾
1931 ST LUCIA XO 4ᵗʰ edition	43				▾
1931 ST LUCIA XO 5ᵗʰ edition	46				▾

ADMIRAL RODNEY

G B Rodney

RODNEY BAY, ON THE WEST OF
ST. LUCIA, IS NAMED IN HONOUR
OF THE VISIONARY ADMIRAL,
SIR GEORGE BRYDGES RODNEY,
WHO FAMOUSLY "BROKE THE
LINE" AND VANQUISHED
THE FRENCH FLEET AT
THE BATTLE OF THE SAINTS
ON APRIL THE 12TH

1782

· ST LUCIA · WEST INDIES · DISTILLERS OF FINE AGED AND BLENDED RUMS · THREE · GENERATIONS OF RUM DISTILLING · ROSEAU VALLEY

ADMIRAL RODNEY

ORIGIN

The rum is a tribute to the English Admiral Rodney, who defeated the French in 1782 in the Battle of the Saints.

FLAVOUR AND AROMA

Made from 100% column still rum, Admiral Rodney is the showpiece of St. Lucia Distillers when it comes to age and complexity.

This rum is matured in used bourbon barrels and the average age in the bottle is approximately twelve years. In time, St. Lucia Distillers want to increase the age to eighteen years as more older rum becomes available for blending.

ENGLISH STYLE

FUNKY   BAKING SPICES

2

FUNKY   BAKING SPICES

FRUITY   FRUITY

FRENCH STYLE   SPANISH STYLE

Name	Alc. %				
Admiral Rodney XO [2]	40				▪

ANGOSTURA

ORIGIN

Angostura is a leading Caribbean rum producer and the market leader in cocktail bitters. It all started with those bitters, back in 1824 when a certain Dr Gottlieb Siebert invented a herbal mixture at his surgery in Angostura as a remedy against fatigue and stomach complaints. In 1875 the family company moved to Trinidad and early in the twentieth century it started blending local rum. Trinidad Distillers was founded in 1949, using a modern multi-column still that gave them a reputation as a producer of top-quality rum. Priced at around 30,000 euros, the Angostura Legacy rum is pretty much the most expensive rum in the world. Luckily, the other variants are much more affordable.

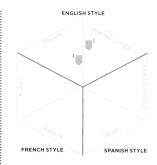

Name	Alc. %				
Angostura Reserva	40				▮
Angostura Gold 5 Years	40				▮
Angostura 7 Years	40				▮
Angostura '1919' 8 Years[4]	40				▮
Angostura '1824' 12 Years[5]	40				▮
Angostura '1787' 15 Years	40				▮
Angostura No. 1	40				▮
Angostura No. 1 French Oak	40				▮
Angostura Siegert's 190	40				▮
Angostura Legacy	40				▮

EXTRA
AGED **12** YEARS
FOR A MINIMUM OF

SINCE 1749

PPLETON ESTATE

AGED **12** YEARS

CREATORS OF   FINE RUMS   *Estate Distilled*

JAMAICA RUM

℮ 70cl

STILLED, BLENDED AND BOTTLED IN JAMAICA BY J.WRAY & NEPHEW LTD.

APPLETON ESTATE

ORIGIN

The Appleton Estate is located in the Nassau Valley in St. Elizabeth, Jamaica. According to the oldest sources, production of rum started here in 1749, but the estate itself goes back to before 1655, when it was owned by Sir Francis Dickinson. The domain has changed owners several times, but the quality standards and the philosophy have always remained the same.

FLAVOUR AND AROMA

All ingredients are from the local terroir. The sugar cane is produced on site and the company has its own fresh-water spring. All the rums are made from molasses and are matured in a specific type of American oak barrel to ensure dominant vanilla tones. The master blender on duty is none other than Joy Spence, the first woman in the world to become a master blender.

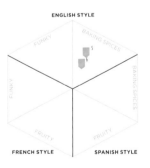

Name	Alc. %	🛢	🌿	🍍	🍶
Appleton Signature Blend [6]	40				🔻
Appleton Reserve Blend	43				🔻
Appleton Rare Blend 12 Years [5]	43				🔻
Appleton 21 Years	43				🔻
Appleton 50 Years	45				🔻

BLACK TOT

ORIGIN

The name Black Tot refers to a black day in the history of rum. At 11 a.m. on 31 July 1970, a 300-year-old naval tradition ended that had provided sailors with a daily rum ration. After that date, the rum was decanted into stone jars and stored in warehouses that were owned by the British government. It spent over 40 years in those jars and was then bought up by Specialty Drinks, which has bottled all the rum and sells it systematically. As you can guess, this rum isn't exactly cheap. Most bottles sell for more than 750 euros.

FLAVOUR AND AROMA

This is the navy rum *par excellence*. Its alcohol content of 54.3% means you really have to be able to take it.

Name	Alc. %				
Black Tot Last Consignment	54.3				

BORGOE®
82

Jubilee Blend

*Superior Suriname
Golden Rum*

Distilled, Blended & Bottled by Suriname Alcoholic Beverages N.V.
Cornelis Jongbawstraat 18-28, Paramaribo, Suriname
www.sabrum.com

38% Alc./Vol.   70cl

BORGOE

ORIGIN

Borgoe is a product of Suriname Alcoholic Beverages NV, which has operated in Suriname in the sugar cane industry since 1882.

FLAVOUR AND AROMA

The rum is based on molasses, distilled in a triple column still. After that, the young alcohol is matured in new American oak barrels. Borgoe 82 was introduced in 1982 to commemorate the centenary of the Mariënburg sugar plantation, from which it derived its name. The showpiece Borgoe 15 Years was introduced to commemorate the forty-fifth anniversary of Suriname Alcoholic Beverages NV in 2011. After the rum has been distilled in an authentic copper pot still, it is imported back from Kentucky, USA, after maturing in oak barrels for fifteen years. In Suriname, Borgoe is the undisputed market leader and the brand has become steadily more popular in the Netherlands over the years.

Name	Alc. %	🛢	🌿	🍍	🍶
Borgoe 82	40				🔵
Borgoe Extra	40				🔵
Borgoe Vintage	40				🔵
Borgoe 8 Years	40				🔵
Borgoe 15 Years	40				🔵

BUNDABERG

ORIGIN

Bundaberg Rum was created when local sugar producers in the small town of Bundaberg were trying to find a way to get rid of their waste material, molasses. The Bundaberg Distilling Company was set up in 1888 and marketed its first rum a year later. The polar bear on the bottle may seem a strange choice for an Australian rum producer. The creators chose the polar bear as their mascot because their rum makes you feel warm no matter how cold it is outside. The company also has a soft drinks production line that produces their ready-mixed *Bundy 'n' Coke*. The company was bought in 2000 by the British multinational company, Diageo, which moved the bulk of the bottling line to Queensland in 2014. Unfortunately, this led to major job losses.

FLAVOUR AND AROMA

After two days of fermentation, for which the company uses its own yeast strain, the molasses are washed in a kind of column still and then distilled in a pot still. The rum is then matured in new American oak barrels for at least two years. The premium range, which is unfortunately very hard to find in Europe, is still made in Bundaberg.

Name	Alc. %	🛢	🌿	🍍	🍾
Bundaberg	37.5				▽
Bundaberg Overproof	57.7				▽

Bundabe
RUM
STILLED, MATURED & BOTTLED AT
ABERG DISTILLING

CAPTAIN MORGAN

ORIGIN

Although Captain Morgan flirts with a rich pirate history for its marketing, the company was actually founded in 1944 by Seagram, one of the largest distillery groups at the time. The recipe was inspired by a family recipe from the Levy Brothers, pharmacists in Kingston. They bought 'raw' rum from the Long Pond Distillery in Jamaica, added herbs and then allowed the mixture to mature. Production was soon moved to Puerto Rico for tax reasons. The brand was purchased in 2001 by the beverage giant Diageo, which commercialised it further.

FLAVOUR AND AROMA

For the production, it uses a mixture of molasses and *mash*. The mash is a mixture of grain and water, which is also used for brewing beer. They do the distillation with a column still, after which the drink is matured in new American oak barrels for a maximum of one year. Finally, herbs and spices are added to create one of the best-known spiced rums. A number of variants are issued worldwide, tuned to suit local tastes. The bulk of the output is currently produced in St. Croix.

Name	Alc. %	🛢	🌿	🍍	🍾
Captain Morgan White	40				▪
Captain Morgan Original Spiced	40		▪		▪
Captain Morgan Jamaica	40				▪
Captain Morgan Black Spiced	40		▪		▪

CARONI

ORIGIN

Trinidad once had fifty distilleries, but by 1950 only eight were left and today only one remains. But between 1923 and 2003 Caroni was undoubtedly the yardstick for rum aficionados. This rum, which arose at the heart of sugar cane plantations in the Caroni Plains, is famous for its heavy style. When the local sugar refinery closed in 2003, leading to a collapse in sugar cane production in Trinidad, it was only a matter of time before the Caroni distillery had to close. One year later, an eccentric Italian by the name of Gianluca Gargano, who worked for the drinks importer Velier, visited the distillery and found various stocks of rums that dated back to the 1970s. He purchased the lot and is currently allowing them to mature further.

FLAVOUR AND AROMA

The Caroni distillery was the last rum producer to use local molasses from Trinidad. As a barrel was only bottled in exceptional circumstances, this is considered one of the most coveted rums on the market. It is a rum for daredevils and rum lovers, because each and every bottle hides an unseen explosion of flavours. The high alcohol content creates an extra rush.

Name	Alc. %	🛢	🌿	🍍	🍶
Caroni 12 Years [15]	50				🛡
Caroni 15 Years	52				🛡
Caroni 18 Years	55				🛡
Caroni 2000 15 Years (The Nectar special edition)	70.4				🛡

CARONI

100% TRINIDAD RUM

aged *15* years

Extra Strong

104° PROOF

CHAIRMAN'S RESERVE

ORIGIN

This is a brand that belongs to the St. Lucia Distillers Group, also known for Admiral Rodney. The rum was first created in 1999 and very soon became a local hit. It has now also gained international recognition and won various awards.

FLAVOUR AND AROMA

The rum combines both pot still and column still distillates that have both matured separately for about five years in used bourbon casks. They are then blended into a whole, after which they are stored for six months in the same barrels. Chairman's Reserve also creates a spiced rum and a white rum, both made largely the same way. However, the white rum is matured and filtered for a slightly shorter period of time. Various spices and fruits are macerated in the spiced rum.

Name	Alc. %	🛢	🌿	🍍	🧴
Chairman's Reserve	40				🔻
Chairman's Reserve White label	40				🔻
Chairman's Reserve The Forgotten Casks	40				🔻
Chairman's Reserve Spiced	40		🔻		🔻

COCKSPUR

ORIGIN

Valdemar Hanschell was a Danish sailor who, in around 1884, settled in Barbados, which had one of the largest seaports in the Caribbean at the time. He started a trading post that supplied ships with food and other goods, such as rum. He was the first to use the recipe for Cockspur rum, which was to become one of the most popular Barbadian rums.

FLAVOUR AND AROMA

Cockspur is made at the West India Rum Refinery, which is next to the beach north of Bridgetown. After a strictly controlled five-day fermentation, the majority of the molasses are distilled in a four-column still up to an alcohol content of 95%. The other fraction is distilled in a pot still up to an alcohol content of around 75%. The result is a lighter and a heavier rum, respectively. The blend of the two is then matured in oak barrels. An extra asset is the water that is used to dilute the rum to make it ready for consumption: the water is filtered through coral and the quality is therefore very high.

Name	Alc. %	🛢	🌿	🍍	🍾
Cockspur Fine Rum	40				▼
Cockspur 12 Years	40				▼

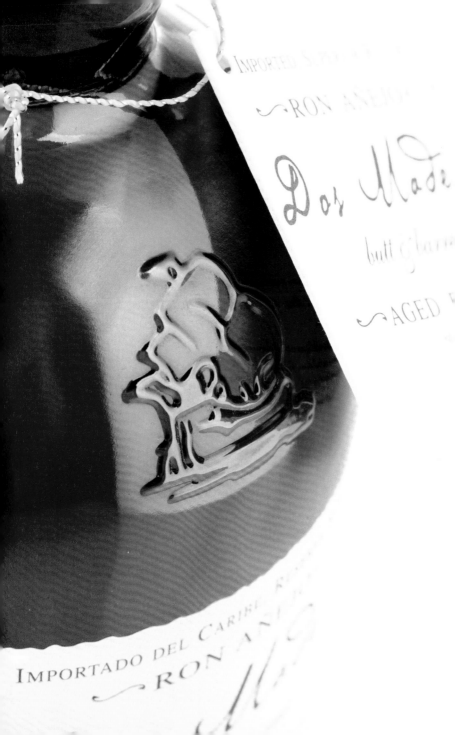

DOS MADERAS

ORIGIN

Why should a rum from Spain stick to an English style? Dos Maderas purchases various rums in Barbados and Guyana, blends them and lets them mature using its own double maturation system.

FLAVOUR AND AROMA

The rum stays in the Caribbean for the first five years, stored in used bourbon barrels. After that the rum goes to Europe, where it is matured for three years in sherry casks that were previously used for maturing Palo Cortado for twenty years. An additional step is included for Dos Maderas 5Y+5Y PX. This rum is matured for another two years in Pedro Ximénez sherry barrels. Their showpiece is the Dos Maderas Luxus, which is matured for ten years, rather than five, and then laid down for five more years in Pedro Ximénez barrels. Purists think that these rums tend too much toward sherry, but we reckon they are definitely worth trying.

Name	Alc. %				
Dos Maderas 5Y+3Y	37.5	▼			▼
Dos Maderas 5Y+5Y PX	40	▼			▼
Dos Maderas Luxus	40	▼			▼

EL DORADO

ORIGIN

Guyana has a rich rum tradition that started around 1640, when the Dutch established the first sugar cane plantations. The English introduced distillation ten years later. Things burgeoned after that, and there were already around 300 distilleries by the beginning of the eighteenth century. The first settlements near the Demerara river arose in 1752; this is where Demerara rum was eventually developed. Each of the various plantations had its own specific still and therefore had a brand mark of its own. They joined forces in 1998 and founded Demerara Distillers Ltd. Today, the distillery has the largest collection of stills that are used to this day, even including some antique wooden column stills and pot stills. El Dorado rum was created in 1992.

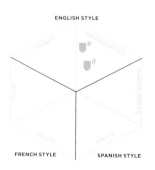

ENGLISH STYLE

FRENCH STYLE   SPANISH STYLE

The rums are blends based on molasses from the various stills. They are matured in used oak barrels in Guyana, where the process is about twice as fast as in cooler regions. The age stated on the bottle is the age of the youngest rum in the blend. Besides the entry-level series, there is also a premium range, a high-end range and a selection of single barrels that you can recognise by the names of the various estates.

Name	Alc. %	🛢	🌿	🍍	🍶
El Dorado White	40				🔵
El Dorado Gold	40				🔵
El Dorado Dark	40				🔵
El Dorado Spiced	40		🔵		🔵
El Dorado Deluxe Silver 6Y	40				🔵
El Dorado 3 Years	40				🔵
El Dorado 5 Years	40				🔵
El Dorado 8 Years	40				🔵
El Dorado 12 Years [22]	40				🔵
El Dorado 15 Years	40				🔵
El Dorado 21 Years [23]	40				🔵
El Dorado 25 Years	40				🔵
El Dorado Single Barrel EHP (Enmore Estate)	40				🔵
El Dorado Single Barrel ICBU (Uitvlugt Estate)	40				🔵
El Dorado Single Barrel PM (Port Mourant Estate)	40				🔵

ELEMENTS 8

ORIGIN

Elements 8 is a young company that was launched in 2006 at the London Bar Show. Its makers have molasses from Guyana distilled by St. Lucia Distillers in three different type of stills: a John Dore pot still, a Coffey column still and a Kentucky Bourbon Vendome pot still. The rum is matured in St. Lucia, in oak bourbon barrels. Key points are that the molasses are cooled down before fermentation and the company uses its own three strains.

FLAVOUR AND AROMA

The Platinum has matured for four years, whereas the Gold has been kept in barrels for six. Both products are blends of more than ten rums. Exotic Spices is a spiced rum, created after about ten different fruits and herbs have macerated in the barrel for two weeks. The Criollo Cacao Rum has matured for three years in Buffalo Trace bourbon barrels to which Criollo cocoa beans were added at intervals.

Name	Alc. %	🛢	🌿	🍍	🍶
Elements 8 Platinum	40	▼			▼
Elements 8 Gold	40	▼			▼
Elements 8 Barrel Infused Exotic Spices	40	▼	▼	▼	▼
Elements 8 Barrel Infused Criollo Cacao Rum	40	▼		▼	▼

ENGLISH HARBOUR

ORIGIN

In 1932, Portuguese rum merchants decided to revive rum production in Antigua. Originally, they marketed the rum under the name of Cavalier. English Harbour was created in 1993, and the focus switched to mature rums when the 5 Years was launched.

Fun fact about the 25 Years: This rum was designed for Antigua's independence celebrations in 1981. Some of the barrels disappeared into oblivion and were only rediscovered during a relocation in 1995. Many of the barrels were still intact, but unfortunately, 75% of the rum had evaporated. The remaining rum was blended together and was kept in the same barrels for another ten years. Maturation finally reached its peak in 2004 and the rum was transferred into steel tanks to stop the interaction with the wood. The pot stills in Antigua were reset and repaired in 1991. That is why this is the only rum that gives you some idea of the original stills.

FLAVOUR AND AROMA

Sugar is no longer produced in Antigua, which is why the molasses are now imported from the Dominican Republic and Guyana. These molasses are fermented for 24 to 36 hours in open tanks and both artificial and natural yeasts are used to achieve this. The wild yeasts, which can be found in nature everywhere, are very important because the distillery is located on the coast. The yeasts give the rum a slightly saline edge. Distillation takes place in one of the last two copper column stills remaining in the Caribbean. Most stills in the Caribbean are made of steel. The rum is matured in used bourbon barrels.

Name	Alc. %	🛢	🌿	🍍	🍾
English Harbour 5 Years	40				▼
English Harbour 10 Years	40				▼
English Harbour 1981 25 Years	40				▼

Aged **5** Years

Fine Caribbean Rum distilled in copper stills...

English Harbour

Aged

FAIR

FAIRTRADE

ORIGIN

Fair is a young brand that started up in 2009 and focuses on fair trade products. Ethical responsibility and quality are its top priorities. In addition to excellent vodka and some top liqueurs, its range also includes three rums.

FLAVOUR AND AROMA

Fair Belize, a rum based on molasses, is distilled in a column still, after which it is matured in bourbon barrels for five years. Fair Belize 10 Years has been matured in a process lasting ten years. The company also has a product from the Worthy Park distillery in Jamaica, which has also been laid down in bourbon barrels for five years.

Name	Alc. %	🛢	🌿	🍍	🧴
Fair Belize	40				🔹
Fair Belize 10 Years	40				🔹
Fair Belize 11 Years	50.7				🔹
Fair Jamaica	40				🔹

GOLD OF MAURITIUS

ORIGIN

The is one of the newest rums, only brought on the market in 2014. This rum, designed by Frederic Bestel, is a product of Litchquor Ltd.

FLAVOUR AND AROMA

Its basis is molasses and it is distilled in the column stills of Grays Ltd. in the west of the island. For the time being, the European market has to settle for the Gold of Mauritius Dark, but the variant that has been matured for five years may yet be marketed there.

Name	Alc. %				
Gold of Mauritius Dark	40				

Gold of Mauritius

DARK RUM

5

GOSLINGS

ORIGIN

James Gosling, the son of a beverage merchant from Kent, headed to the Far West in 1806 with about 10,000 pounds worth of goods on board. After a journey of around 91 days he was forced to moor in Bermuda. He opened a shop together with his brother Ambrose and that business kept going for no less than 127 years. The first barrels of matured rum arrived in Bermuda in 1857, and after a lot of experiments the Gosling brothers managed to create a blend of their own that would later become known as Black Seal. Goslings Black Seal is one of the few spirits that have managed to obtain copyright for a cocktail of their own: in the States, a 'Dark & Stormy' can only be made using this rum and Goslings Ginger Beer.

FLAVOUR AND AROMA

Where the rum is made and exactly what goes into it are still a secret. What we do know is that the Goslings use both a pot still and a column still for all their rums. They always give the same answer when asked how long they mature their rum: 'As long as it needs.' The Family Reserve is said to have been matured for the longest of all rums.

Name	Alc. %				
Goslings Gold Seal	40	▣			▣
Goslings Black Seal	40	▣			▣
Goslings Black Seal 151 Overproof	75.5	▣			▣
Goslings Family Reserve Old Rum	40	▣			▣

GREEN ISLAND

ORIGIN

This Mauritian rum has been around since 1960 and still has the same packaging and the same label. The basis of the rum is molasses. It is distilled four times and then matured in oak barrels.

FLAVOUR AND AROMA

The Superior Light is a blend of rums between three and five years old that are run through a charcoal filter to remove their colour.

Local fruits and herbs are added to the Spiced Gold. Flamboyant Vieux is a golden rum, blended from rums up to seven years old. Fun fact: The flamboyant, which blooms in March, the month Mauritius gained independence, can be seen as the national tree of Mauritius.

Name	Alc. %	🛢	🌿	🍍	🍾
Green Island Superior Light	40				🛡
Green Island Spiced Gold	37		🛡		🛡
Flamboyant Vieux 7 Years	40				🛡

GREEN ISLAND

SPICED

-GOLD-

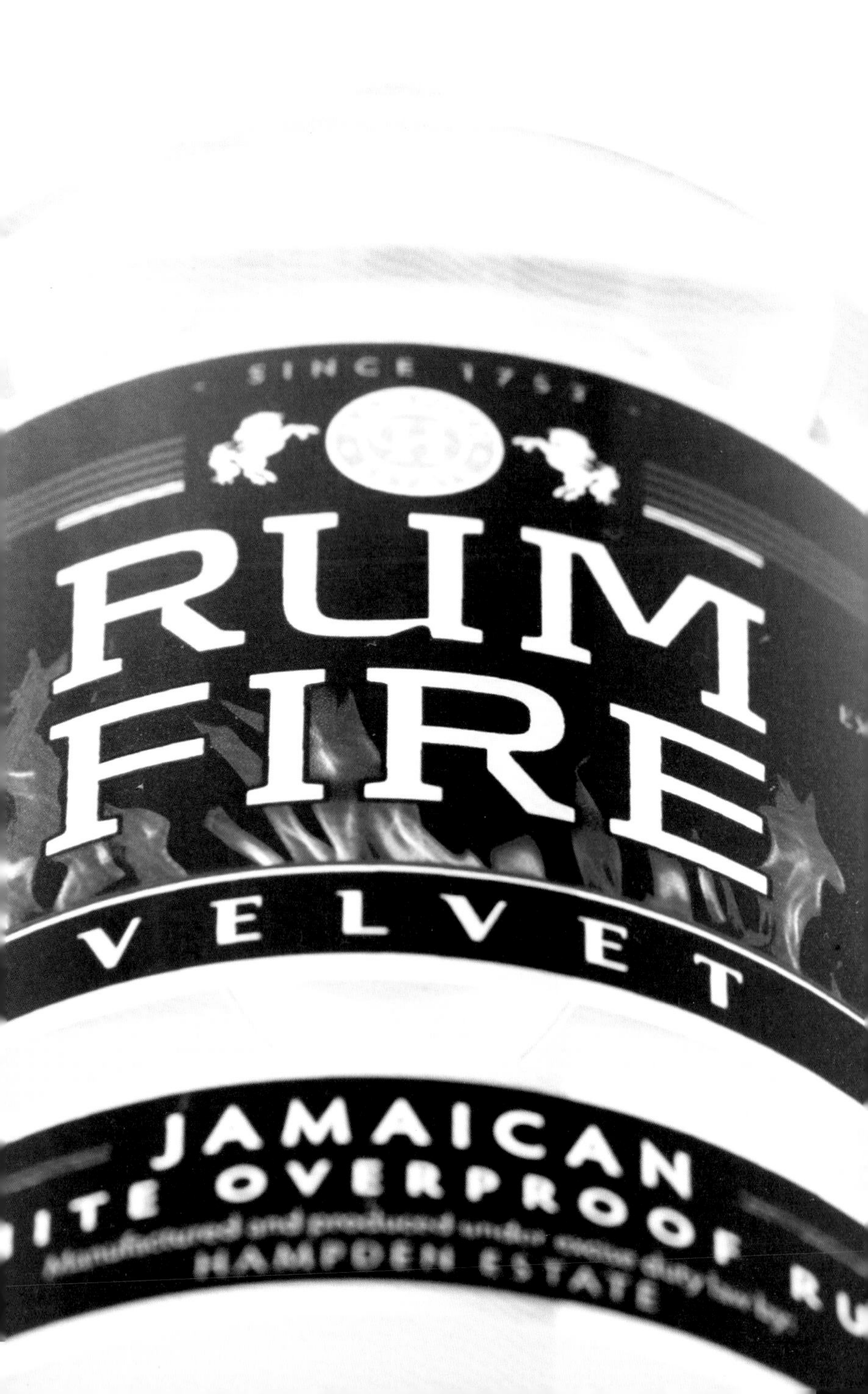
RUM
FIRE
VELVET
JAMAICAN
HAMPDEN ESTATE

HAMPDEN ESTATE

ORIGIN

Hampden Estate, founded in 1753, is the only Jamaican distillery that specialises in heavy pot-stilled rums with prominent esters. It mostly produces rum that is used in blends by other brands, but it also has a few variants of its own.

FLAVOUR AND AROMA

Rum Fire is based on Trelawny JB, an extremely popular rum that could only be obtained clandestinely until Rum Fire was launched. Because its rum has a lot of esters and is therefore very aromatic, Hampden Estate is also an important producer for the perfume industry.

Name	Alc. %				
Rum Fire Velvet Overproof	63				
Hampden Gold	40				

JEFFERSON'S 1785 EXTRA FINE DARK RUM

ORIGIN

The Jefferson family started doing business around 1734, but did not start producing rum on the island of Antigua until fifty years later. They were also the supplier for the White Star Line, the shipping company that built the Titanic.

FLAVOUR AND AROMA

The rum that we know under this name today is based on a recipe from 1785. This company purchased pot-stilled rum in Jamaica and Guyana (Demerara) and transported it to Liverpool, where it was blended and allowed to mature further. It is not known how long the rum is matured.

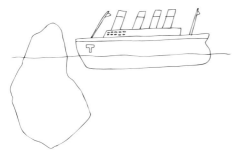

Name	Alc. %	🛢	🌿	🍍	🍶
Jefferson's 1785 extra fine dark rum	40	▼			▼

JEFFERSON'S

Extra Fine
DARK RUM

SUPERIOR IMPORTED
CARIBBEAN RUM

1785

ESPECIALLY BOTTLED BY RSM SOLUTIONS NE LTD FOR
R&R JEFFERSON, LOWTHER STREET, WHITEHAVEN, CUMBRIA

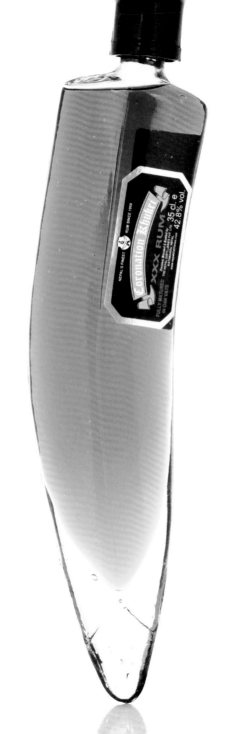

KHUKRI

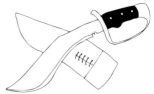

ORIGIN

Since its foundation in the 1950s, Nepal Distillery Pvt. Ltd. (NDPL) has been a front runner in spirits. The distillery is located in Kathmandu, which has a rather cool climate and also has local spring water.

The company made its first small forays into distillation with pot stills: their design was based on patents from 1870. Those pot stills are no longer used today, although they are still on display. The company currently uses modern three-column stills in which the molasses are distilled into rum. After that, the rum is matured in wooden barrels for at least eight months.

FLAVOUR AND AROMA

Khukri XXX is the most popular rum in Nepal and has an 80% share of the local market. However, we mainly know this as Khukri Coronation, which is sold in a dagger-shaped bottle. There is also a Khukri Spiced on the market, flavoured with local fruits and spices.

Name	Alc. %	🛢	🌿	🍍	🍾
Khukri XXX	42.8				▼
Khukri Spiced	43		▼	▼	
Khukri Coronation	42.8				▼

KRAKEN BLACK SPICED RUM

ORIGIN

The kraken is a mythological creature from exciting pirate stories. It looks like a gigantic octopus or squid, hence the image on the label of the rum. However, this rum is a very recent product, designed by Proximo Spirits. This American beverage giant has ambitions to market a cocktail/long drink of its own called the Perfect Storm, using its own rum combined with its in-house ginger beer, Kraken Storm. Are they planning a competitor for the patented Dark & Stormy from Goslings?

FLAVOUR AND AROMA

This spiced rum from 2010 is based on rum from Trinidad & Tobago. Kraken Rum is matured in oak barrels for twelve to twenty-four months, after which it is blended with thirteen spices that include ginger, cinnamon and cloves. A Kraken Black Spiced Rum with an alcohol content of 40% is on the market in Belgium and the Netherlands; there is also a 47% variant in other countries such as the United States.

Name	Alc. %				
Kraken Black Spiced Rum	40				

RUM

The
KRAKEN

BIZARRE & FIERCE
Sea Creatures
As seen through the eyes
of imagination

The

EST.
1849

LAMB'S

IMPORTED

GENUINE

NAVY RUM

LAMB'S NAVY RUM

ORIGIN

In 1849, Alfred Lamb, the son of beverage merchant William Lamb, got inspired by the British navy's rum history and decided to blend eighteen rums from Guyana, Barbados, Trinidad and Jamaica into a new navy rum. After blending, the rum was kept in oak barrels at a warehouse near the Thames for four years. The brand is now owned by the largest independent beverage manufacturer in the United Kingdom, Halewood International.

FLAVOUR AND AROMA

Lamb's is a dark, traditional navy rum. In other words, a rum with a strong flavour.

Name	Alc. %				
Lamb's Navy Rum	40				

LEMON HART

ORIGIN

Lehman ('Lemon') Hart was the grandson of a beverage importer from Cornwall in the EN who imported rum from the Caribbean. Inspired by his grandfather, Lemon Hart created a unique blend of rums from the Demerara Valley in Guyana, eighty years after grandfather Abraham Hart had started the family business. This blend led to Lemon Hart becoming the official supplier of rum to the British Royal Navy. The brand continued to exist until Black Tot Day, the day that the last ration of rum was distributed by the Royal Navy. In 2010, the Canadian company Mosaiq Inc. purchased the brand name from Pernod Ricard to revive the authenticity of the brand.

FLAVOUR AND AROMA

Today, Lemon Hart is once again a blend of 100% Demerara rums that have been matured in Guyana. The best-known type is the Lemon Hart 151, a 75.5% overproof rum that is often used in tiki cocktails.

Name	Alc. %	🛢	🌿	🍍	🍶
Lemon Hart Original	40				🔻
Lemon Hart 151 Overproof	75.5				🔻
Lemon Hart Navy Spiced	43		🔻		🔻

MOUNT GAY

ORIGIN

The oldest source mentioning this distillery dates back to 1703, making this the oldest rum in the world. Mount Gay Distilleries is currently owned by the Remy Cointreau beverage group.

The name comes from Sir John Gay Alleyne, the right-hand man of John Sober, who owned the Mount Gilboa plantation and distillery from 1747. Sir John Gay Alleyne immediately took over the day-to-day management of this plantation. However, a Mount Alleyne already existed, so Sir John's middle name was chosen instead and Mount Gay was born!

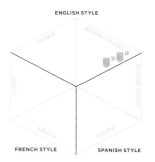

FLAVOUR AND AROMA

Distillation still takes place in the old double pot stills, in which molasses that have been fermented in the open air are processed into alcohol. The rum is matured in used American whiskey barrels. All the rums are blends of more than ten separate distillates. To create Mount Gay Black Barrel, the rum is transferred after the first maturation into extra roasted bourbon barrels, which creates an even more spicy effect.

Name	Alc. %	🍺	🌿	🍍	🍶
Mount Gay Silver	40				▼
Mount Gay Eclipse	40				▼
Mount Gay Black Barrel	40				▼
Mount Gay XO [30]	40				▼
Mount Gay 1703 [29]	40				▼

MOUNT GILBOA

TRIPLE DISTILLED

BARBADOS

POT STILL RUM

PRODUCED BY
MOUNT GILBOA INVESTMENTS LTD.

MOUNT GILBOA

ORIGIN

Mount Gilboa is the original name of the plantation where Mount Gay is currently located. According to managing director Frank Ward, there had never been any intention to change the name of the plantation from Mount Gilboa to Mount Gay. However, while people were performing the formalities after the sale of the plantation, the rum was flowing a bit too freely and the names ended up being filled in incorrectly on the forms!

FLAVOUR AND AROMA

This rum comes from the same pot stills and barrels as Mount Gay. But the big difference is in the distillation method. Mount Gay is distilled twice in different copper pot stills, whereas Mount Gilboa is distilled three times in the refinery's copper pot still. So this rum gives you an idea of how the spirit must have tasted two hundred years ago. Production of this rum was stopped because it was not very successful. This was also partly due to the fact that the bottle did not look attractive, giving the impression that you had bought the rum at a supermarket.

Name	Alc. %				
Mount Gilboa Pot Still Rum	40				▢

JAMAICA

MYERS'S ORIGINAL DARK

ORIGIN

The brand is owned by beverage giant Diageo. The product is a blend of pot still and column still rum. After distillation, the rum is matured in new oak barrels for up to four years.

FLAVOUR AND AROMA

Myers's is one of the few rums that add the used molasses to the end product again, which may largely explain its dark colour.

Name	Alc. %	🛢	🌿	🍍	🍾
Myers's Original Dark	40	▼		▼	▼

00% FINE JAMAICA

WORLD

F

MYERS
RUM

Original D

NEW GROVE

ORIGIN

The production of rum in Mauritius only really got off the ground when Dr Pierre Charles Harel decided to process and distil sugar cane at his gigantic estate in Pample-mousses. Grays Distillery has been located near this estate since 1932. It also makes various other products for the local market in addition to New Grove.

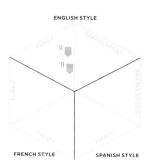

FLAVOUR AND AROMA

The column stills at Grays Distillery process fermented molasses into rum, which is matured in used French limousin barrels. Nearly all the matured rums have exactly the age stated on the bottle, except for the New Grove 21 Years, which was matured using the solera system, and of which only around 700 bottles were made. Hardly any additives are used; only the New Grove Dark contains a bit of caramel for the colour.

New Grove has also experimented with double maturation since 2015. After maturing in classic French oak barrels, the batch is blended and transferred into three unusual types of barrels: this results in three types of rum, each with its own flavour. The first, the Moscatel, is matured in barrels that contained sweet dessert wine. The second is the Acacia, which uses wood from the acacia tree. The third type is the Merisier, which uses barrels of wood from the sweet cherry tree.

Name	Alc. %	🛢	🌿	🍍	🍾
New Grove Silver	37.5				🔵
New Grove Dark	37.5				🔵
New Grove Spiced	37.5		🔵		🔵
New Grove Plantation [31]	40				🔵
New Grove Oak Aged	40				🔵
New Grove 5 Years [32]	40				🔵
New Grove 8 Years	40				🔵
New Grove 21 Years	40				🔵
New Grove Double Cask Acacia	47				🔵
New Grove Double Cask Moscatel	47				🔵
New Grove Double Cask Merisier	47				🔵

OLD JAMAIQUE

ORIGIN

Long Pond Estate, where this molasses-based rum was made, was owned by the beverage giant Seagram's at the time of the distillation: the company also had Captain Morgan made there. Today this distillery is owned by the Jamaican government.

FLAVOUR AND AROMA

You may wonder what the point is of allowing a rum to mature for thirty years or more. This is indeed a waste of time in warmer climates. However, this rum was distilled in Jamaica and then matured in bourbon barrels in the warehouses of the Scotch whisky bottler Ian MacLeod in Broxburn.

Name	Alc. %	🛢	🌿	🍍	🍾
Old Jamaique 30 Years	50				◗
Old Jamaique 35 Years	50				◗

OLD MONK

ORIGIN

The precursor of Old Monk is the Hercules rum that was only destined for the Indian army and did not have a good reputation. Connoisseurs who have drunk both confirm that Old Monk is an enormous improvement in terms of quality.

Until 2013, this was the most popular rum worldwide, selling eight million bottles a year. Recent relaxation on Indian import legislation means that the market share is collapsing now that big players such as Bacardi also have access to the market.

FLAVOUR AND AROMA

The rum, based on molasses, is made in a column still. The standard variant has matured in oak barrels for at least seven years, whereas the Supreme has been laid down for twelve. The Supreme is sold in a monk-shaped bottle.

Name	Alc. %				
Old Monk	42.8				
Old Monk Supreme	42.8				

PUSSER'S RUM

ORIGIN

Rum and the sea are inextricably connected with each other, but no single rum has such a close relationship with the sea as Pusser's. This is because *pusser* was the nickname for the purser, the ship's logistics officer. In the past, the sailors were given their daily portion of rum by the purser until this was abolished in 1970. But in 1979, a certain Charles Tobias wanted to revive this custom, so he started Pusser's Ltd. in the Virgin Islands. His first blend was, in his own words, based on the original recipe of the rum that was served on board the ships.

Fun fact: Today, Pusser's Rum donates part of the money that it receives from the worldwide sales of Pusser's Rum to the Royal Navy Sailors' Fund, which is also known as the Tot Fund.

FLAVOUR AND AROMA

Pusser's is a powerful, spicy navy rum that demands respect. The complexity and character of Pusser's Rum Aged 15 Years can compete with the best brandies and cognac.

Name	Alc. %	🍶	🌿	🍍	🍾
Pusser's Rum Original Admiralty Blend (Blue Label) [39]	40	▪			▪
Pusser's Rum Gunpowder Proof (Black Label)	54.5	▪			▪
Pusser's Rum Overproof (Green Label)	75	▪			▪
Pusser's Rum Aged 15 Years	40	▪			▪
Pusser's Rum Spiced	35	▪			▪

PYRAT RUM

ORIGIN

Pyrat Rum is owned by Patron Spirits, a company that was founded by John Paul DeJoria and Martin Crowley in 1989. Patron Spirits does not have a distillery of its own, but selects various rums that are blended into their Pyrat Rum. When the brand was set up in 1997, the rum was produced by the Anguilla Rums Company, which stored a selection of various rums in the Caribbean. Production was recently transferred to Guyana in South America.

FLAVOUR AND AROMA

The rum is very successful internationally and is characterised by aromas of citrus, vanilla and cinnamon. The rum consists of a blend of various rums, which vary in age from eight to forty years old. The rum is matured in French oak using the solera system.

CITRUS   CINNAMON   VANILLA

Name	Alc. %				
Pyrat Rum XO Reserve	40				

FINE AGED
CARIBBEAN RUMS

WWW.PYRATRUM.COM

PYRAT RUMS

PYR
RUM

XO RESERVE

700ml

40% vol.

R.L. SEALE & COMPANY

ORIGIN

R.L. Seale & Company has existed as rum bottlers and rum merchants since 1920, but it was not until 1995 that David Seale took over a refurbished sugar factory. He had stills installed there that he designed himself, and started producing rum a year later. The distillery is therefore one of the newest and most modern in the Caribbean. The Foursquare Distillery can perform vacuum distillation, which runs at lower temperatures and retains more flavour. The company is now run by the master blender and master distiller Richard Seale, David's son.

The Foursquare Distillery has a pot still and a column still, and both are used for the production. Maturation takes place in old bourbon barrels. After maturing in bourbon barrels for five years, Doorly's XO is finished in used Oloroso sherry barrels.

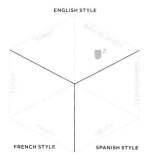

FLAVOUR AND AROMA

R.L. Seale's 10 Years is the brand name used in Europe for Old Brigand. This no-nonsense rum is a little experiment by Richard Seale and has a unique dry aftertaste, making it very popular with whisky fans. The Foursquare Port Finish is also a pot still and column still blend, but the unique aspect is that it has been kept in port barrels for six of the nine years of maturation, whereas the blend is usually only kept in port barrels for a few months. The rum is only marketed in Europe, in an edition of 12,000 bottles. Its range also contains a spiced rum made from rum that has matured for two years in bourbon barrels, to which tropical spices and fruits have been added. No sugar syrup is added to it, in contrast to most other spiced rums.

Name	Alc. %	🛢	🌿	🍍	🍶
Doorly's 3 Years White	40				▮
Doorly's 5 Years Gold	40				▮
Doorly's XO Sherry Finish [21]	40				▮
Doorly's 12 Years	40				▮
R.L. Seale's Old Brigand 10 Years	43				▮
Foursquare Spiced Rum 2 Years	35		▮		▮
Foursquare Port Finish 9 Years	40				▮
Foursquare 11 Years Zinfandel Cask	43				▮
Foursquare Criterion	56				▮

SEA WYNDE

ORIGIN

Sea Wynde combines the best of both worlds. It is not only one of the few distilleries that still use the traditional pot still technique, it is also the only one that combines pot-stilled rums from Jamaica and Guyana.

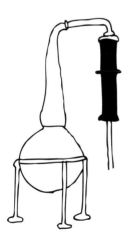

FLAVOUR AND AROMA

Rum was produced in pot stills for centuries. But although you can create fuller flavours using pot stills, many distilleries have chosen to switch to column stills over the course of time. The reason for this is that this method allows them to produce much larger quantities in less time. Sea Wynde combines pot-stilled rums from Jamaica and Guyana to obtain more complexity. The rum is then matured in small oak barrels, partially in the Caribbean and partially in Great Britain. The blend is always bottled in limited quantities, which may cause slight fluctuations in the flavour.

Name	Alc. %				
Sea Wynde Pot Still Rum	46	▮			▮

SIXTY SIX

ORIGIN

Sixty Six rum is made by one of the last independent family businesses in the Caribbean. The rum is distilled, matured and bottled at the Foursquare Rum Distillery in Barbados. This distillery has been owned by the Seale family since 1820 and it is still producing a fantastic premium rum to this day.

FLAVOUR AND AROMA

The Sixty Six Family Reserve rum is a small batch rum (usually 112 barrels), which is 'tropically' matured for at least twelve years in American white oak. Tropical maturation is the makers' way of saying that spirits mature more quickly in the Caribbean than in Europe. After maturation for twelve years, the rum has attained a degree of maturity and complexity comparable to European spirits that are twice as old.

Name	Alc. %	🍷	🌿	🍍	🍾
Sixty Six Family Reserve	40				▊

SMITH & CROSS
LONDON

TRADITIONAL JAMAICA RUM

SMITH & CROSS

ORIGIN

The Smith & Cross brand originates with England's oldest producers of sugar and distilled drinks. The history of the brand dates back to 1788, to a sugar factory in Thames Street in London. Over time, the company became an important trading house for Jamaican rum. Today, this brand is in the portfolio of the well-known Hayman Distillers, the producers of Hayman's Gin.

FLAVOUR AND AROMA

Smith & Cross is a typical Jamaican rum, which is bottled in the United Kingdom. The rum is overflowing with flavours, with dominant exotic fruits and spices.

Name	Alc. %				
Smith & Cross Traditional Jamaican Rum Navy Strength [45]	57				

THE DUPPY SHARE

ORIGIN

The Duppy Share was designed by the Westbourne Drinks Company in London. This small producer has created a blend of high quality rums from the Worthy Park Estate in Jamaica and the Foursquare distillery in Barbados.

FLAVOUR AND AROMA

We are familiar with the term angels' share in the maturation of rum. And there is another portion of the rum that is allegedly lost in a different way: In Caribbean folklore, *duppy* are spirits or ghosts that swoop between the islands stealing the best parts of the rum, hence the name Duppy Share.

Name	Alc. %				
The Duppy Share	40				

THE PINK PIGEON

ORIGIN

This rum derives its name from a rare bird on the island of Mauritius. The makers claim that their single-estate rum is as rare as the Mauritian pigeon.

CITRUS

VANILLA

ORCHID FLOWER

FLAVOUR AND AROMA

The sugar cane that they use comes from their Medine Estate plantation located between the mountains and the sea. The quality is exceptional. The Medine Distillery is the oldest distillery on the island and rum has been made there since 1926. It is also bottled on site. Pink Pigeon is not matured, so as to retain the natural pot-stilled flavour. It is infused with a unique blend of three botanicals: hand-picked bourbon vanilla, citrus and orchid flower petals.

Name	Alc. %				
The Pink Pigeon	43				

The
PINK
PIGEO
·ORIGINA
THE MEDINE DISTILL

TIKI LOVERS

ORIGIN

Tiki Lovers is a creation from The Bitter Truth, a recently founded company (2006) which specialises in bitters, as the name suggests.

FLAVOUR AND AROMA

Tiki Lovers has a white and a dark variant. The bottle reminds you of a tropical bar on some hidden island. Tiki Lovers White Rum is made with pot-stilled Jamaican rum that has matured for three to five years, after which it is filtered and finally mixed with column still rum from Trinidad. The dark variant has an alcohol percentage of 57% and is therefore much stronger. It is also based on matured Jamaican rum, but is mixed with rums from Barbados, Trinidad and Guyana.

Name	Alc. %	🥃	🌿	🍍	🍶
Tiki Lovers White Rum	42	🔵			🔵
Tiki Lovers Dark Rum	57	🔵			🔵
Tiki Lovers Pineapple	45	🔵		🔵	🔵

VIRGIN GORDA

ORIGIN

Virgin Gorda rum is distilled by The Posh-
makers, a distillery in London – also known
for its *ish gin* – that was founded in 2010. The
rum is a blend of various rums from Barbados,
Trinidad and Jamaica.

VANILLA

FLAVOUR AND AROMA

Virgin Gorda is distilled
in a pot still and matured
in American bourbon
barrels. Additives are
not used, making Virgin
Gorda a 100% natural rum.
The rum from Trinidad
gives it fresh tones and a
vanilla character. Jamaica
provides the body because
molasses are used, and
Barbados gives the final
blend a powerful woody and
mature character.

Name	Alc. %				
Virgin Gorda British Caribbean Rum	40				

IRGI
OR

WRAY & NEPHEW

LONDON · 1862   JAMAICA · 1891   PARIS · 1878

White

OVERPROOF RUM

GUARANTEED FULL STRENGTH

Blended and bottled by

J. WRAY & NEPHEW LTD

DISTILLERS & BLENDERS (SINCE 1825)
KINGSTON, JAMAICA, W.I.

e 70 cl   63% vol

WRAY & NEPHEW

ORIGIN

Wray & Nephew is produced by J. Wray & Nephew, the oldest company in Jamaica and one of the largest exporters in the Caribbean. J. Wray & Nephew Ltd. is an important agricultural and industrial company that operates from three estates in Jamaica, namely Appleton, Holland and New Yarmouth. The company's key activities are growing sugar cane, producing sugar, distilling rum and other spirits, and producing wine.

FLAVOUR AND AROMA

Wray & Nephew White Overproof Rum is without a doubt the company's most important brand, and its alcohol percentage of 63% makes it a serious powerhouse that can hold its own in numerous exotic cocktails.

ENGLISH STYLE

FUNKY BAKING SPICES

FUNKY BAKING SPICES

FRUITY FRUITY

FRENCH STYLE   SPANISH STYLE

Name	Alc. %				
Wray & Nephew White Overproof Rum [48]	63				▉

 **XM**

ORIGIN

This rum brand is owned by Banks DIH Ltd. (not to be confused with Banks rum), a local giant in the Guyanese food sector.

FLAVOUR AND AROMA

XM stands for eXtra Mature: each rum from its range is therefore matured. The barrels that it uses are very diverse: new barrels, used sherry barrels, bourbon barrels etc. The various products are then blended.

Name	Alc. %	🛢	🌿	🍍	🧴
XM 5 Years d'Aguilar's	40				🔵
XM VXO 7 Years	40				🔵
XM Royal 10 Years	40				🔵
XM Millenium 12 Years	40				🔵
XM Supreme 15 Years	40				🔵

12
YEAR OLD

XM

SPECIAL BLEND

Millennium
R U M

Demerara's Finest

70cl

40%
Alc./Vol.

BLENDED, BOTTLED & EXPORTED BY
BANKS DIH LIMITED
© AQUIAR'S INDUSTRIES & HOLDINGS

RHUM BIELLE

2002

Marie Galante

FRENCH STYLE

These rums are made from fresh sugar cane sap, as you can tell from the taste. They retain the original flavour of the sugar cane. They are elegant and often slightly more expensive than the rums that are produced from molasses. During maturation, the *ouillage* technique (see also 'Maturation process') is often used.

COUNTRIES

Martinique, Guadeloupe, Marie-Galante, Haiti, French Guyana, Réunion

BASIC PRODUCT

Pure sugar cane juice

PRODUCTION METHOD

Column still (except for rhum agricole from Haiti)

FLAVOUR AND AROMA

Fruity, intense, floral, earthy, complex, elegant

ARCANE

ORIGIN

Mauritius is not in the Caribbean, but it is known for its climate, which is perfectly suited for growing sugar cane and therefore for rum production. Arcane always uses sugar cane juice as the basis and therefore many consider it a rhum agricole.

FLAVOUR AND AROMA

Its range comprises four products: Cane Crush, Delicatissime Gold, Extraroma 12 Years Amber and the spiced rum Beach House Spiced. Arcane Cane Crush is a white rum that has been distilled twice, the first time in a copper pot still in Mauritius and the second time in traditional alembics in the French Cognac region. Delicatissime Gold is a young golden rum that has been matured in oak barrels for eighteen years. Extraroma 12 Years has been matured using the solera system. As mentioned earlier, there is also a spiced rum besides the Arcane range: Beach House Spiced, in which local fruits and spices have been incorporated.

Name	Alc. %	🍶	🌿	🍍	🧴
Arcane Cane Crush	43.8				
Arcane Delicatissime Gold	41				🔹
Arcane Extraroma 12 Years Amber	40				🔹
Beach House Spiced	40		🔹		

Appellation
Martinique Contrôlée

RHUM VIEUX
AGRICOLE
MARTINIQUE

J.BALLY

12

ANS D'ÂGE

Martinique

Le Carbet

45% Vol.   70cl

Habitation Lajus • 97221 Le Carbet • Martinique • France

J. BALLY

ORIGIN

Although the distillery has been closed since 1989, rum is still produced and bottled under this brand name. Most old vintage rums from Martinique are named J. Bally.

The brand itself was created in 1924. It can easily be recognised by the tapered square shape of the bottle and the original label. After its closure in 1989, the column still was transferred to Distillerie Simon.

Tip: If you come across a bottle, look at the year of bottling as well as the year of distillation. A 1964 rum, for instance, may have matured for only three years, whereas other rums from the same year have been kept in the barrel for longer.

FLAVOUR AND AROMA

Inspired by the production techniques used for cognac, this French style rum has a very dry taste. Fermentation is short – only 72 hours. The sugar cane is selected on the basis of the sugar content. To ensure optimum quality, the company restricts its harvesting to the months of January and February.

Name	Alc. %				
J. Bally 7 Y Vieux	45	▮			
J. Bally 12 Y Vieux	45	▮			
J. Bally Millésime 2002	43	▮			

HAITI

BARBANCOURT

ORIGIN

In 1862, Dupré Barbancourt, a Frenchman from the Charente, completed the rum that still bears his name today. After his death, his wife took over the company together with his nephew, Paul Gardère. Today, the company is led by the fourth generation of Gardères. Initially, the rums that had matured the longest were reserved exclusively for friends and family. But the international ambitions shifted when the distillery moved to the heart of the Domaine Barbancourt in the middle of the twentieth century.

FLAVOUR AND AROMA

The basis of the rum distillate is molasses. Dupré was always inspired by cognac, which is why he used a double distillation method. Using this method, he managed to create a unique and delicate rum, which breaks away from the classic vegetal tones of a rhum agricole.

ENGLISH STYLE

FRENCH STYLE   SPANISH STYLE

Name	Alc. %				
Barbancourt White	43				
Barbancourt 3 Star 4 Years	43				▮
Barbancourt 5 Star 8 Years [9]	43				▮
Barbancourt 15 Years Gran Reserve	43				▮

MAISON FONDÉE EN 1862

AGED 4 YEARS

VIEILLI 4 A

★★★ ★★★

Rhum
Barbancourt®

RHUM de CANNE à SUCRE 100% SUGAR CANE RUM

VIEILLI en FÛT de CHÊNE - OAK AGED

HAITI

 BIELLE

ORIGIN

Marie-Galante, which is also known as "the island with a hundred mills", has always been a sugar cane island. Distillerie Bielle dates back to the end of the nineteenth century and uses the rhum agricole principle. The distillery is located on the Bielle Plateau, 110 metres (360 ft) above sea level.

FLAVOUR AND AROMA

During the 1940s it produced 26,000 litres of rum with an alcohol content of 50%. Today it produces 330,000 litres of rum with an alcohol content of 59%. This rum is matured in oak barrels and finished in used cognac barrels.

ENGLISH STYLE

FUNKY · BAKING SPICES

FUNKY · BAKING SPICES

FRUITY · FRUITY

FRENCH STYLE · SPANISH STYLE

Name	Alc. %	🛢	🌿	🍍	🍾
Bielle Blanc	59				
Bielle Ambre	50				▮
Bielle 2002	52.8				▮
Bielle 2003	52.9				▮
Bielle 2004	45				▮
Bielle 2006 [1]	42				▮
Bielle 2007	57.3				▮

CHARRETTE

ORIGIN

The name Charrette arose in 1972 and was a combination of three distilleries from La Réunion that dated back to the beginning of the eighteenth century. The intention was to produce a rum that symbolised the island of La Réunion. Eighty per cent of the rum produced here is intended for the island itself and the rest is exported, mainly to France.

FLAVOUR AND AROMA

The rum is a blend of the rums from each of the three producers, Distillerie Savanna, Distillerie Rivière du Mât and Distillerie Isautier. The rum is based on both molasses and sugar cane juice, which is unusual for this region. Maturation takes place in French oak barrels.

Name	Alc. %	🛢	🌿	🍍	🍾
Charrette Traditionnel	49				🍶
Charrette Ambré	40				🍶
Charrette Vieux 3Y	40				🍶
Charrette Vieux 5Y	40				🍶
Charrette Vieux 7Y	40				🍶

Rhum Charrette

ILE DE LA RÉUNION

RHUM VIEUX
TRADITIONNEL DE LA RÉUNION

3 ANS

MARTINIQUE

CLÉMENT

ORIGIN

In 1887, the physician Homère Clément bought Domaine de l'Acajou, a 43 hectare sugar cane plantation in Martinique. This rhum agricole pioneer opened a distillery in 1917 to meet the demand for rum during the war. His son Charles took over the company after his death and launched the brand name Clément in 1940. Today, Clément is one of the big names in rhum agricole and it is available in more than sixty countries.

ENGLISH STYLE

FRENCH STYLE   SPANISH STYLE

FLAVOUR AND AROMA

After harvesting, the sugar cane is squeezed within the hour to retain the freshness of the juice. This juice is then fermented for 48 to 72 hours in stainless steel tanks, for which the brewer's own yeast and natural yeasts are used. After that, the mixture is distilled in a copper column still, designed as a copy of the old French Armagnac still. Finally, the rum is slowly diluted to give a more palatable alcohol content and, if necessary, laid down to mature in a mixture of American oak barrels and limousin barrels. Clément also regularly launches special editions and single casks, which have sometimes been matured in unique ways.

Name	Alc. %	🛢	🌿	🍍	🍾
Clément Blanc	40				
Clément Blanc	50				
Clément Blanc	55				
Clément Canne Bleue	50				
Clément Ambré	40				█
Clément Vieux	44				█
Clément Vieux VSOP [16]	40				█
Flamboyant Vieux 6 Years	44				█
Clément Vieux 10 Years	44				█
Clément Cuvée Homère	44				█
Clément Single Cask Bourbon Barrel	46.8				█

DAMOISEAU

ORIGIN

At the end of the nineteenth century, a certain Mr Rimbaud from Martinique started the Bellevue Distillery in the town of Le Moule. In 1942, it was bought by Roger Damoiseau, the founder of the Rhum Damoiseau. Today, the company is led by his grandson Hervé Damoiseau. Damoiseau has a fifty per cent market share of rum locally and exports to over forty countries.

FLAVOUR AND AROMA

Sugar cane juice from the first pressing is used as the basis. Distillation is carried out in the same way as for French Armagnac brandy. After distillation, the rum is transferred into used bourbon barrels.

The climate in Guadeloupe means that the angels' share is high: 1 litre of ten-year-old rum requires two litres of unmatured spirits. Therefore, half of it is lost. White rum is also matured for six months before being bottled.

Name	Alc. %	🛢	🌿	🍍	🝪
Damoiseau Blanc	40				
Damoiseau Blanc	55				
Damoiseau Vieux	42				🝪
Damoiseau VSOP	42				🝪
Damoiseau XO	42				🝪
Damoiseau 1953	42				🝪

DEPAZ

ORIGIN

The history of this brand dates back to 1651, twenty years after the French colonists first set foot in Guadeloupe, Saint-Martin, Saint-Barthélemy and of course Martinique. The Mont Pelée volcano erupted in 1902 and the plantation and distillery were destroyed. Victor Depaz, the only family member who survived, returned to the region in 1917 to rebuild everything. He succeeded, and distillation of rum began again.

FLAVOUR AND AROMA

The sugar cane juice used for distillation comes from the 'Canne Bleue', a type of sugar cane that is more difficult to grow than others, but has a higher sugar content.

Name	Alc. %	🛢	🌿	🍍	🍶
Depaz Blanc	50				
Depaz Blanc	55				
Depaz Vieux	45				▼

DeSilver

WHITE RUM WITH
SECRET SPICES
FROM ST-BARTH

70 CL   40% VOL.

St-Barth - French West Indies

DESILVER

ORIGIN

This recent rum owes its name to Captain DeSilver, a bloodthirsty pirate from the seventeenth century who – legend has it – had a rum of his own, made with secret spices. A nice marketing story, but this spiced rum has already genuinely captured a few prizes.

FLAVOUR AND AROMA

DeSilver is one of the few spiced white rums. The spices come from Saint-Barthélemy. Unfortunately, little is known about the distillate.

Name	Alc. %				
DeSilver White	40		▮		

 # DILLON

ORIGIN

Like many rum brands in Martinique, the history of Dillon dates back to the seventeenth century. Various members of the family played minor roles in the American War of Independence and the French Revolution.

FLAVOUR AND AROMA

Using the method that is typical for rhum agricole, the sugar cane juice is fermented briefly and then distilled in a column still. After a short resting period in steel tanks, the white rum is bottled or transferred into oak barrels for maturation.

Name	Alc. %				
Dillon Blanc	43				
Dillon Blanc	50				
Dillon Blanc	55				
Dillon Vieux	43				▯
Dillon Très Vieux	43				▯
Dillon XO	43				▯
Dillon Grenadier	43				▯
Dillon Dark Cigar Réserve	40				▯

RHUM
DILLON
DARK RUM

Dillon i bon

DISTILLERIE
DILLON

RHUM 1972 VIEUX

RHUM VIEUX

DOMAINE DE

Courcelles

(GRANDE-TERRE · GUADELOUPE)

Vieux Rhum de Sucrerie distillé en Janvier 1972
Eleveé en fût de 220 litres,
mis en bouteille en Juin 2011

70cL   54,3% vol.

DOMAINE DE COURCELLES

ORIGIN

The Courcelles distillery closed around 1960, but the stills were used until 1972. The rums were only bottled some forty years later and are therefore real collector's items. They are still available, but extremely popular because of their great age.

Tip: Always check the exact date of bottling on the bottle label to know whether you are getting a bargain. There's not much chance of finding a bottle for under 150 euros.

FLAVOUR AND AROMA

This rum is matured in small 220-litre barrels, which means more contact with the wood and it emphasises flavour tones such as vanilla and butterscotch. However, the vegetal character that is so typical of the French style is retained.

Name	Alc. %				
Domaine de Courcelles 1972	42				▮

HSE

ORIGIN

HSE, the abbreviation for Habitation Saint-Etienne, started off in the early nineteenth century as a sugar plantation. In 1882, the plantation got a fully-fledged distillery when Amédée Aubéry purchased the plantation. It was owned by the Simonet family for most of the twentieth century, but went downhill during the 1980s. The current owners, Yves and José Hayot, bought the domain in 1994 and relaunched the HSE brand, which makes rum according to the original tradition.

FLAVOUR AND AROMA

This rum, like any rhum agricole, uses sugar cane juice as the basis. After a brief period of fermentation, the sugar cane wine is distilled into 73% alcohol in a column still. The rum is then either diluted until it is ready for consumption or matured.

HSE has a very extensive range. Besides classic white rum in various strengths and matured rums of various ages, it also offers various millésimés, special finishes and special editions. Each type has its own specific maturation process, but they are all matured in new French oak barrels first.

Name	Alc. %	🛢	🌿	🍍	🍾
HSE Blanc	50				
HSE Blanc	55				
HSE Blanc Cuvée 2012	50				
HSE Elevé sous bois	42				▮
HSE VO	42				▮
HSE VSOP [26]	45				▮
HSE XO	43				▮
HSE Islay Finish	44				▮
HSE Highland Finish	44				▮
HSE Oloroso Finish	45				▮
HSE Sauternes Finish	41				▮
HSE Pedro Ximénez Finish	46				▮
HSE Porto Finish	42				▮
HSE Black Sheriff	40				▮
HSE Blanc Cuvée Titouan Lamazou	40				▮
HSE Single Cask Extra Vieux 2003	47.8				▮
HSE Small Cask Vieux 2004	46				▮
HSE Hors d'Age 1960	45				▮

 KARUKERA

ORIGIN

Karukera is produced by Hope Distillery, the oldest distillery on the island of Guadeloupe. Karukera is the original name that the Caribbean people gave to the island.

FLAVOUR AND AROMA

The entire production chain takes place on the island, from planting the sugar cane to the final rum in the bottle. The basis of this typical rhum agricole is, of course, sugar cane juice, which is then distilled in column stills and matured in oak barrels. Single casks and other variants are also marketed in addition to the standard range.

Name	Alc. %	🎚	🌿	🍍	🍾
Karukera Silver	40				
Karukera Gold	40				🔹
Karukera Blanc Canne Bleue	50				
Karukera Vieux [27]	42				🔹
Karukera Millésime 2000	50.8				🔹
Karukera Millésime 1999	45				🔹
Karukera Millésime 1997	46.3				🔹
Karukera Cuvée Christophe Colomb Hors d'Age	45				🔹
Karukera Réserve Spéciale	42				🔹
Karukera 2000 Single Cask - Sauternes Cask Finish	46.5				🔹

LA MAUNY

ORIGIN

Ferdinand Poulain, Count de Mauny, arrived in Martinique in 1749, where he married the daughter of a southern plantation owner. From then on, the plantation was known as the Domaine de La Mauny. Besides sugar, it also produced tafia, a precursor of rum. When the sugar economy threatened to grind to a halt around 1820, the domain switched entirely to producing rhum agricole. A new column still and steam machines were purchased in 1929 and production was modernised.

FLAVOUR AND AROMA

After a short 24-hour fermentation, the sugar cane juice is distilled in three different column stills until an alcohol content of 65%-75% is reached. It is then blended and diluted until it is ready for consumption, or rested in oak barrels to mature. The amber rums have matured in barrels for at least eighteen months.

Name	Alc. %				
La Mauny	40				
La Mauny	50				
La Mauny	55				
La Mauny Spicy Mauny	32		🛡		
La Mauny VO	40				🛡
La Mauny VSOP	40				🛡
La Mauny XO	40				🛡
La Mauny 1998 Vintage	42				🛡
La Mauny Ruby	42				🛡
La Mauny Saphir	40				🛡

DEPUIS 1749
LA MAUNY

LONGUETEAU

ORIGIN

When the sugar crisis broke out in earnest at the end of the nineteenth century, the Marquis de Sainte-Marie had accumulated substantial gambling debts. To settle them, he sold his domains to Henri Longueteau, who converted the old refinery into a distillery in 1895. The domain is still owned by this family today and it is fully self-sufficient in raw materials.

Sugar cane juice is used and distilled in a large column still in the rhum agricole style. The company, like most producers of French-style rum, has an extensive range of white rums that are excellently suited to a Ti'Punch, for instance.

The matured rums are laid down in used brandy barrels for at least eighteen months. The age stated on the bottle is the age of the youngest rum in the blend.

Name	Alc. %	🍺	🌿	🍍	🫗
Longueteau Blanc	40				
Longueteau Blanc	50				
Longueteau Blanc	55				
Longueteau Blanc	62				
Longueteau Ambré	40				🔸
Longueteau Original Spicy	40		🔸		
Longueteau 3 ans	42				🔸
Longueteau 6 ans	42				🔸
Longueteau VS	42				🔸
Longueteau VSOP	42				🔸
Longueteau XO	42				🔸
Longueteau Grande Reserve Millésime 2004	42				🔸

MONTEBELLO

ORIGIN

Montebello is a rum from Distillerie Carrere in Petit-Bourg, Guadeloupe. The domain has its own sugar cane plantation, but at fifteen hectares, the estate is too small to provide sufficient sugar cane juice for the production volume of 700,000 litres of rum. That is why sugar cane juice is also purchased from other farmers. The majority of the rum produced is exported to France.

The distillery was established in 1930 and has been owned by Gregory Marsolle, now the third generation of Marsolles, since 2012.

FLAVOUR AND AROMA

Unlike the other rums from Guadeloupe, Montebello is less floral and has a much stronger flavour of citrus and sugar cane.

The sugar cane is pressed by two different mills that are driven by a steam engine dating from 1880. The sugar cane juice is then fermented in tanks for thirty hours before being distilled into alcohol in one of the two column stills. The blend is matured in American oak barrels.

Name	Alc. %				
Montebello Blanc	50				
Montebello Ambré	50				▮
Montebello Vieux 4 Years	42				▮
Montebello Très Vieux Rhum 6 Years	42				▮
Montebello Hors d'Age 8 Years	42				▮
Montebello Hors d'Age 10 Years	42				▮
Montebello Hors d'Age 11 Years	42				▮
Montebello Hors d'Age Millésime 1999	40				▮
Montebello Hors d'Age Millésime 1982	42				▮
Montebello Hors d'Age Millésime 1948	47				▮

NEISSON

ORIGIN

The story of Neisson Rhum starts in 1931, when the distillery was set up by the brothers Adrien and Jean Neisson. Today the company is run by Jean's grandson. It is one of the newest distilleries on the island.

ENGLISH STYLE

FUNKY · BAKING SPICES

FUNKY · BAKING SPICES

31

FRUITY · FRUITY

FRENCH STYLE · SPANISH STYLE

FLAVOUR AND AROMA

The sugar cane is pressed within three hours of being harvested to ensure as little loss of flavour as possible. After that, the juice is fermented slowly for seventy-two hours. Distillation takes place in an old copper Savalle column still until an alcohol content of 75% has been reached. The rum is then kept in steel tanks for six months before it is bottled. The matured rums are laid down in limousin barrels for at least eighteen months.

L'Esprit de Neisson was created for the first time on the occasion of the distillery's seventieth anniversary. This product comes directly from the Savalle still, which has to be specially adjusted every time for this rum. With an alcohol content of 70%, this rum should not be underestimated!

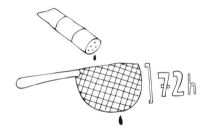

Name	Alc. %	🍯	🌿	🍍	🛢
Neisson Blanc	50				
Neisson Blanc	52.5				
Neisson Blanc	55				
Neisson L'Esprit De Neisson [3]	70				
Neisson Réserve Spéciale	42				🛢
Neisson Extra Vieux	45				🛢
Neisson Fût Unique 2004	42.7				🛢
Neisson 15 Years	44.7				🛢
Neisson 18 Years	43.6				🛢
Neisson 21 Years	45.3				🛢
Neisson Cuvée du 3ème Millénaire	45				🛢

PÈRE LABAT

ORIGIN

Père Labat rum has been produced by the small Poisson distillery for more than a century. The name comes from a renowned French missionary and engineer, Jean-Baptiste Labat, who modernised the sugar industry in the French Antilles at the end of the seventeenth century. However, Père Labat never set foot on Marie-Galante...

This is the oldest distillery on the island, and it still has a few treasures from the past, such as an old copper pot still and a steam-operated sugar cane press. Though nowadays, production is to modern standards using column stills.

FLAVOUR AND AROMA

Marie-Galante has the perfect climate for growing sugar cane, which also guarantees its superior quality. It certainly helps give the rum its aromatic character.

Name	Alc. %	🛢	🌿	🍍	🍾
Père Labat Blanc	40				
Père Labat Blanc	50				
Père Labat Blanc	59				
Père Labat Doré	50				▮
Père Labat 3 Ans Vieux	42				▮
Père Labat 8 Ans Très Vieux	42				▮
Père Labat 1985	42				▮
Père Labat 1997	42				▮

RHUM JM

ORIGIN

The story of Rhum JM began in 1914, when Gustave Crassous de Médeuil purchased the JM distillery from Jean-Marie Martin. The family has kept to the same traditional working methods ever since.

FLAVOUR AND AROMA

The sugar cane juice that is used comes from the Habitation Bellevue plantation. The rum is made in a column still and matured in bourbon barrels that were charred again for this purpose. The distillery uses the ouillage technique, in which the angels' share is topped up with rum from the same year.

The brand recently launched a special series: rums that were distilled in 2005 and finished in barrels of the popular French spirits calvados, cognac and armagnac.

Name	Alc. %	🍾	🌿	🍍	🫙
JM Blanc	50				
JM Blanc	55				
JM matured in wood	50				🫙
JM VO	43				🫙
JM VSOP	43				🫙
JM XO	45				🫙
JM Hors d'Age Edition Limitée	42%				🫙
JM Hors d'Age Cognac Finish	40.5				🫙
JM Hors d'Age Calvados Finish	40.8				🫙
JM Hors d'Age Armagnac Finish	41.5				🫙

MARIE-GALANTE

RHUM RHUM

ORIGIN

In 2004 Luca Gargano – yes, the same eccentric Italian we came across in the Caroni rum item – sent a certain Gianni Capovilla to Marie-Galante with the task of creating the world's best rhum agricole. Gianni lived up to the challenge and installed the first alembic in the Bielle distillery in 2005. A second alembic followed two years later and the first bottle of Rhum Rhum was ready one year after that.

FLAVOUR AND AROMA

Marie-Galante has always been a sugar cane island and still has types of sugar cane that have disappeared elsewhere. It is the mixture of these various types of sugar cane that makes Rhum Rhum so unique.

ENGLISH STYLE

FUNKY · BAKING SPICES · BAKING SPICES · FUNKY · FRUITY · FRUITY

40

FRENCH STYLE   SPANISH STYLE

Name	Alc. %	🛢	🌿	🍍	🧴
Rhum Rhum Blanc Agricole	41				
Rhum Rhum Blanc Agricole [40]	56				
Rhum Rhum Libération 5 Ans	45				🛢
Rhum Rhum Libération 5 Ans	59.8				🛢

MARIE-GALANTE

RHUM RHUM

ORIGIN

In 2004 Luca Gargano – yes, the same eccentric Italian we came across in the Caroni rum item – sent a certain Gianni Capovilla to Marie-Galante with the task of creating the world's best rhum agricole. Gianni lived up to the challenge and installed the first alembic in the Bielle distillery in 2005. A second alembic followed two years later and the first bottle of Rhum Rhum was ready one year after that.

FLAVOUR AND AROMA

Marie-Galante has always been a sugar cane island and still has types of sugar cane that have disappeared elsewhere. It is the mixture of these various types of sugar cane that makes Rhum Rhum so unique.

ENGLISH STYLE

FUNKY · BAKING SPICES · FUNKY · BAKING SPICES · FRUITY · FRUITY

40

FRENCH STYLE   SPANISH STYLE

Name	Alc. %				
Rhum Rhum Blanc Agricole	41				
Rhum Rhum Blanc Agricole [40]	56				
Rhum Rhum Libération 5 Ans	45				🛢
Rhum Rhum Libération 5 Ans	59.8				🛢

RIVIERE
DU MÁT

ILE DE LA REUNION

RHUM

RHUM RIVIÈRE DU MÂT

ORIGIN

Rhum Rivière du Mât is produced by La Maison Rivière du Mât, one of the oldest and most important distilleries in the island. The company produces no less than 80,000 litres of rum every day. The distillery controls every stage of production and offers a wide range of rums.

FLAVOUR AND AROMA

The delicate and spicy rums are the result of hard work and traditional craftsmanship that has been passed down from generation to generation. When creating rum, the brand relies upon the oenologist Christian Vergier, as a way of getting the best from the terroir. The rums are characterised by overtones of pepper and chili.

Name	Alc. %				
Rivière du Mât Blanc	50				
Rivière du Mât Traditionnel Vieux 3 Years	45				🥃
Rivière du Mât Grande Réserve 6 Years	40				🥃
Rivière du Mât XO	42				🥃
Rivière du Mât Vintage 2014 10 Years	43				🥃

SAINT AUBIN

ORIGIN

The Saint Aubin plantation is in the south of Mauritius and has been operational since 1819. The plantation still bears the name of its first owner, Pierre de Saint Aubin.

FLAVOUR AND AROMA

The sugar cane is still harvested manually today, after which it is immediately pressed at the factory. Saint Aubin only uses the juice from the first pressing for its rum production. The juice is then fermented and distilled in a traditional copper alembic. The company only uses spring water from the Bois Chéri tea plantation.

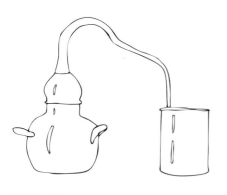

Name	Alc. %				
Saint Aubin 1819 White Agricultural Rum	50				
Saint Aubin 1819 Vanilla Rum	40			▢	
Saint Aubin 1819 Coffee Rum	40			▢	
Saint Aubin 1819 Spiced Rum	40		▢	▢	
Saint Aubin 1819 Historical Collection – Old Grand Port Battle	40				▢
Saint Aubin 1819 Aged Rum 5 Years	40				▢

SAINT JAMES

ORIGIN

Saint James was founded in secrecy in 1765 by Reverend Father Edmond Lefébure, who led the Brothers of Charity monastery. At the time, the Brothers of Charity ran the hospital at Fort Saint-Pierre, which could host up to 500 patients, soldiers and needy people. Father Lefébure, the leader of the congregation, had a sugar factory set up for the needs of the hospital in Trou-Vaillant. Traditionally, this also required a vinegar distillery, where the syrupy residues of the molasses were distilled into a kind of alcohol. The quality of the raw alcohol was dubious, but Father Lefébure managed to improve it with the help of other monks until a fully-fledged spirit was created.

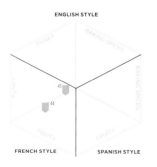

FLAVOUR AND AROMA

Today this distillery is, as they say in Martinique, a company that 'is smoking', i.e. an active operation. The Saint James rum is created by fermenting and distilling pure sugar cane juice. This rum therefore meets the strict standards of the designation of origin as *Rhum Agricole Martinique*, the only AOC rum in the world. Distillation at a low temperature in a column still is a preparation method that is only used in the French Antilles and it is what gives Saint James rum its strongly aromatic tone and fruity flavour.

Name	Alc. %	🍶	🌿	🍍	🛢
Saint James Impérial Blanc [43]	40				
Saint James Royal Ambré	40				🛢
Saint James Vieux Agricole	42				🛢
Saint James Hors d'Age [44]	43				🛢
Saint James 7 Years	43				🛢
Saint James 12 Years	43				🛢
Saint James 15 Years	43				🛢
Saint James Cuvée 1765	42				🛢
Saint James Quintessence	42				🛢

TAKAMAKA BAY

ORIGIN

The Takamaka Bay rum is produced by the Trois Freres Distillery, a distillery that was started by the brothers Richard and Bernard d'Offay in 2002. The brothers' dream was to create a rum based on a recipe that they had inherited from their grandfather. Takamaka Bay Dark Rum was their first offering, followed later by a white rum, a coconut rum and a vodka. Their mission: to produce the Indian Ocean's best rum.

The rum is distilled three times: the first time in a pot still, the second and third time in a column still. The rum is then kept in stainless steel tanks for three months, after which it is matured in new American oak barrels. The makers of the Takamaka Bay say that they are also experimenting with used port barrels and bourbon barrels. For their coconut rum they use a natural coconut extract that is added to the rum in the stainless steel tanks. The spiced rum is aromatised with caramel, vanilla and other local spices.

Name	Alc. %	🛢	🌿	🍍	🍶
Takamaka Bay White Rum	38				
Takamaka Bay Dark Rum	38				▮
Takamaka Spiced Rum	38		▮		
Takamaka Bay Overproof Rum	72				▮
Takamaka Bay Coco Rum	25			▮	
Takamaka Bay St. André Rum Vesou	40				
Takamaka Bay St. André 8 Year Old Rum	40				▮

TROIS RIVIÈRES

ORIGIN

Trois Rivières is a rhum agricole from Martinique. It was produced by Distillerie Trois Rivières from 1785 to 2004. The brand was then transferred to La Mauny Distillerie, which is owned by BBS. Trois Rivières has been part of the French Groupe Chevrillon since 2012. The original distillery was bordered by three rivers, the Bois d'Inde, the Oman and the St. Pierre. The rum's name (French for 'three rivers') was therefore an obvious choice.

Trois Rivières is known for its full flavour and has had the AOC Martinique (Appellation d'Origine Contrôlée) label since 1996.

Name	Alc. %				
Trois Rivières Rhum Cuvée Spéciale Mojito & Longdrink	40				
Trois Rivières Rhum Blanc Agricole	40				
Trois Rivières Rhum Blanc Agricole [47]	50				
Trois Rivières Rhum Blanc Agricole	55				
Trois Rivières Rhum Cuvée de l'Océan	42				
Trois Rivières Rhum Ambré [46]	40				▯
Trois Rivières Cuvée Du Moulin	40				▯
Trois Rivières VSOP Réserve Spéciale	40				▯
Trois Rivières Triple Millésime 1998-2000-2007	42				▯
Trois Rivières Cask Strength Millésime 2006	55.5				▯
Trois Rivières 12 Years Old	42				▯
Trois Rivières Millésime 1995	43				▯
Trois Rivières Millésime 2000	43				▯

WILLIAM HINTON

ORIGIN

The Portuguese island of Madeira was one of the first areas where sugar cane was grown intensively. In the sixteenth century, Madeira was in fact the largest sugar exporter in what was then the known world. However, it was not until the nineteenth century that sugar cane was effectively processed into rum.

One of the pioneers was William Hinton, a British merchant, who invested heavily in sugar cane. In addition to rum production, he also manufactured furniture made from sugar cane leaves and canes. He built the first distillery in 1845, which makes rum that is largely based on the French style.

FLAVOUR AND AROMA

The sugar cane juice is pressed and distilled once in a column still. William Hinton 3 Years is matured in French oak barrels for three years.

Name	Alc. %				
William Hinton White	40				
William Hinton 3 Years	40				🔻
William Hinton 6 years	42				🔻
William Hinton 6 years Whisky Cask	42				🔻
William Hinton 6 years Madeira Cask	42				🔻
William Hinton 6 years Brandy Cask	42				🔻
William Hinton 6 years Sherry Cask	42				🔻
William Hinton 6 years Port Cask	42				🔻

William Hinton®
RUM
RUM FROM MADEIRA ISLAND
PRODUCT OF PORTUGAL
EST. 1845
Madeira
Island
RUM AGRÍCOLA DA MADEIRA
700ML
40% VOL
William Hinton®
RUM
RUM FROM MADEIRA ISLA
AGED 3 YEARS
PRODUCT OF PORTUGAL
EST. 1845
Madeira
Island
RUM AGRÍCOLA DA MADEIRA
700ML
40% VOL

SPANISH STYLE

These are usually light rums with a clean taste. They were relatively late in conquering the rum market. Spanish-style rums often use the solera system. The age on the bottle is generally an average of the rums used, not the age of the oldest rum.

COUNTRIES
Cuba, Puerto Rico, Dominican Republic, Venezuela, Guatemala, Nicaragua, Panama, Colombia, Peru, Costa Rica, Ecuador

BASIC PRODUCT
Molasses

PRODUCTION METHOD
Short fermentation – column still

FLAVOUR AND AROMA
Buttery, rounded, sweet

PANAMA

 ABUELO

ORIGIN

The history of the Varela Hermanos dates back to 1908, when Don José Varela Blanco, a young Spanish immigrant, started the first sugar refinery in Panama, which had just gained independence. At the insistence of his three sons, he started distilling sugar cane juice in 1936. The company now has a 90% share of the local market. Until a few years ago it also produced for Bacardi, but now it focuses entirely on Ron Abuelo.

FLAVOUR AND AROMA

The basis of this rum is virgin honey, an extract from the first phase of pressing, which is distilled in column stills. The rum is matured in bourbon barrels and all bottles are blends; the label states the oldest rum.

Name	Alc. %				
Abuelo Añejo	40				🬛
Abuelo 7 Years [1]	40				🬛
Abuelo 12 Years	40				🬛
Abuelo XV Oloroso	40				🬛
Abuelo XV Napoleon	40				🬛
Abuelo XV Tawny	40				🬛
Abuelo Centuria 30 Years	40				🬛
Abuelo Reserva de la Familia	40				🬛

BACARDI

ORIGIN

Bacardi was originally a Cuban rum brand. The family business sells over 200 million bottles of spirits every year in more than a hundred different countries. Bacardi's main office is currently in Hamilton, Bermuda.

Bacardi was started by Facundo Bacardí on 4 February 1862 in Santiago de Cuba. The brand has had a turbulent history. Various senior executives fled Fidel Castro's regime during the 1960s. The assets of the company in Cuba were nationalised in 1960. In 1992, the various producing companies in Mexico, Puerto Rico, the United States, the Bahamas and Bermuda were merged to form a single company. Today, it is one of the largest drinks groups in the world.

Bacardi has not been active in Cuba since its nationalisation process. Spirits that are made in the former Bacardi distillery are sold under the name Caney. Although Bacardi has nothing to do with Cuba anymore, it still tries to emphasise its Cuban roots for commercial reasons. This is also a result of growing competition in the international rum market.

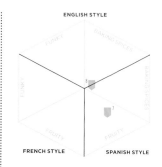

Molasses are used as the basis for the rum, and the distillate is made in column stills. The rum is matured in American oak barrels. Bacardi claims that it still uses its own yeast strain for fermentation, the Levadura Bacardi, which guarantees the consistent taste.

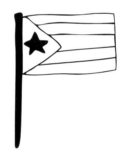

Name	Alc. %	🛢	🌿	🍍	🧴
Bacardi Carta Blanca [8]	40				🛢
Bacardi Carta Oro	40				🛢
Bacardi Carta Oro	40				🛢
Bacardi 151	56.4				🛢
Bacardi Oakheart	35		🛢		🛢
Bacardi 1909 Superior Heritage Limited Edition	44.5				🛢
Bacardi 8 Años [7]	40				🛢
Bacardi de Maestros de Ron, Vintage, MMXII	43				🛢
Bacardi Reserva Limitada	40				🛢

BARCELÓ

ORIGIN

Rum Barceló was created in 1929 by the young Spanish entrepreneur Julian Barceló. The company very quickly grew into one of the largest and most prestigious companies in the Dominican Republic. The distillery is in San Pedro de Macorís. The company has also exported to Europe since the 1990s and is one of the market leaders in its category.

FLAVOUR AND AROMA

Initially, molasses were used for the basic product, but Barceló switched to fresh sugar cane juice a few years ago. Distillation is done in a three-column still, up to an alcohol content of 96%. The rum is matured in American oak barrels.

ENGLISH STYLE

FUNKY · BAKING SPICES

FUNKY · BAKING SPICES

FRUITY · FRUITY

FRENCH STYLE · SPANISH STYLE

Name	Alc. %	🛢	🌿	🍍	🍾
Barceló Añejo	37.5				🔹
Barceló Gran Añejo	37.5				🔹
Barceló Imperial [10]	37.5				🔹
Barceló "30" Aniversario	43				🔹

SP BOTRAN

ORIGIN

The volcanic soil of Guatemala is perfect for growing sugar cane. The Botran family have been active in the sugar cane industry since the end of the nineteenth century, but only started focusing on the production of rum in 1939.

FLAVOUR AND AROMA

The company uses virgin honey as the basis, the extract from the first pressing. It is then distilled in column stills. What makes Botran special is the maturation. The solera system is used, but the high mountains in Guatemala also mean that the angels' share can be minimised. This gives the flavours more time to develop. The year on the bottle refers to the oldest rum in the solera blend. Botran also produces rum that is used for Zacapa, another well-known brand from Guatemala.

ENGLISH STYLE

FUNKY · BAKING SPICES · BAKING SPICES

FUNKY

FRUITY · FRUITY

FRENCH STYLE · SPANISH STYLE

Name	Alc. %				
Botran Reserva Blanca	40				⬤
Botran 12 Years	40				⬤
Botran 15 Years	40				⬤
Botran Solera 1893 18 Years [12]	40				⬤

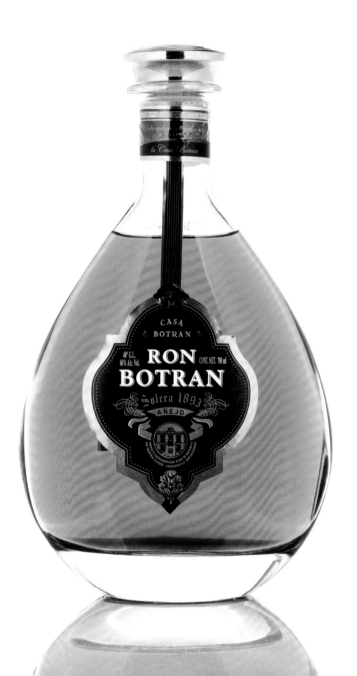

BRUGAL

ORIGIN

Brugal, Bermudez and Barceló, all rums from the Dominican Republic, are the "three Bs". However, Brugal is the undisputed market leader in the Dominican Republic. The company was founded by Don Andrés Brugal in 1888 and has not changed its working methods for over 125 years. The company has three distilleries on the island, one in Puerto Plata and two in San Pedro de Macorís. Although part of the company was taken over in 2008 by Edrington, the Scottish distillers' group, the management is still handled by the family.

FLAVOUR AND AROMA

The company uses molasses as the basis. The liquor is distilled twice in a column still and then matured in selected oak barrels.

Name	Alc. %	🍶	🌿	🍍	🔶
Brugal Especial Extra Dry	40				🔶
Brugal Añejo 5 Years	38				🔶
Brugal Extra Viejo	38				🔶
Brugal 1888 [1]	40				🔶

CACIQUE

ORIGIN

Cacique is a Venezuelan rum brand that was created in 1959 and belongs to Diageo, a British multinational beverages company. It is the undisputed market leader in Venezuela. The word cacique means 'chief' and comes from the old indigenous languages, Taino and Arawak.

FLAVOUR AND AROMA

The rum is made from molasses, distilled three times and then matured in new oak barrels.

Name	Alc. %	🛢	🌿	🍍	🍾
Cacique Añejo	37.5				▾
Cacique 500	40				▾
Cacique Antiguo	40				▾

RON AÑEJO SUPERIOR

ACIQUE

CUBA

SP CANEY

ORIGIN

Although Caney has only existed since 1962, the distillery has been located in Santiago de Cuba since 1862. It was built by Facundo Bacardí. When the Cuban Revolution broke out in 1959, the Bacardi family fled abroad. Its buildings and stocked barrels were nationalised by Castro.

FLAVOUR AND AROMA

The basis of the rum is molasses that comes from sugar cane in the tropical south of Cuba. Not so much is known about the exact working method, except for the fact that distillation still takes place according to the original recipe. The age on the bottle is the age of the youngest rum in the blend.

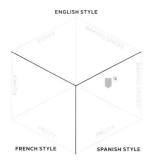

Name	Alc. %	🛢	🌿	🍍	🅞
Caney Blanco 38%	38				▮
Caney Carta Blanca (3Y)	38				▮
Caney Oro Ligero (3 to 5Y)	38				▮
Caney Añejo (min 5Y)	38				▮
Caney Añejo Centuria (min 7Y) [14]	38				▮
Caney Añejo Gran Reserva (min 10Y)	38				▮
Caney 12 Years	38				▮

CARTAVIO

ORIGIN

The area around Cartavio where this rum originates was conquered by Captain Don Domingo de Cartavio in 1675. That feat lives on in the name of the town, Cartavio. Cartavio rum dates from 29 April 1929, when Destilerías Unidas was founded.

FLAVOUR AND AROMA

The rum is matured in old barrels from various countries such as France, Scotland, Spain, the United States and elsewhere. However, Cartavio first chars the casks. The rums are evaluated each year and blended by the master blender; each year the new quality standard is used for the following year. It is said that the solera system is only used for the 12 Years and the XO.

Name	Alc. %	🛢	🌿	🍍	🍾
Cartavio Blanco	40				🍾
Cartavio	40				🍾
Cartavio Black	40				🍾
Cartavio 3Y	40				🍾
Cartavio Selecto 5Y	40				🍾
Cartavio 7 Years	40				🍾
Cartavio 12 Years Solera	40				🍾
Cartavio XO (18Y)	40				🍾

CENTENARIO

ORIGIN

Very little is known about the history of the brand, and the company is also very secretive about its recipe.

FLAVOUR AND AROMA

Although it is highly unusual for a Spanish-style rum, this one is not made from molasses but rather from sugar cane juice. It is the only Costa Rican rum made this way. The rum is matured in used American oak bourbon barrels using the solera system. The flavour is typical of the Spanish style: very clean, buttery and soft.

Name	Alc. %				
Centenario 5Y Añejo Especial	40				▮
Centenario 7Y Añejo Especial	40				▮
Centenario 9Y Conmemorativo	40				▮
Centenario 12Y Gran Legado	40				▮
Centenario Fundación 20 años	40				▮
Centenario 25Y Gran Reserva	40				▮
Centenario 30Y Edición Limitada	40				▮

 **CRUZAN**

ORIGIN

Rum has been produced at the Cruzan distillery for more than 250 years. Cruzan is the term for someone from Saint Croix. The motto of the company and its founders, the Nelthropp family, is "Don't hurry", intended to encourage rum aficionados to unwind and savour every sip.

FLAVOUR AND AROMA

The molasses-based sugar wine is distilled in a five-column still, in the style of familiar Cuban and Spanish rums, to obtain the cleanest spirit possible.

Name	Alc. %	🍶	🌿	🍍	🧴
Cruzan Aged White	40				🧴
Cruzan Aged Dark	40				🧴
Cruzan Aged Dark 151	75.5				🧴
Cruzan Blackstrap	40			🧴	🧴
Cruzan 9 Spiced	40		🧴		🧴
Cruzan Estate Diamond 2 Years	40				🧴
Cruzan Estate Diamond White (5Y)	40				🧴
Cruzan Estate Diamond Dark (5Y)	40				🧴
Cruzan Clipper	40				🧴
Cruzan Single Barrel	40				🧴

CUBANEY

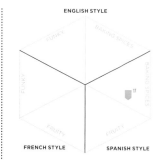

ORIGIN

After Juanillo Oliver, a Catalan, had completed his military service in 1868, he settled in the idyllic town of Las Placetas in Cuba. Initially he grew sugar cane and tobacco, but finally extended his operations to cover the full sugar industry, in which rum production is an important element. However, all the farms and factories were destroyed in 1898 during the War of Independence. Juanillo and his family had to start all over again... and then it was all destroyed a second time during Castro's revolution in 1959. The family left Cuba and split up. During the 1980s some of their descendants returned to Cuba in search of their past. There they discovered old family recipes from the nineteenth century and they decided to continue the tradition. The topography and climate of the Dominican Republic turned out to be nearest to that of Cuba, and with the help of Cuban immigrants and master blenders they managed to restart production.

Not much is known about the production, but we can assume that this rum is made from a sugar wine based on molasses that is distilled in a column still in San Pedro de Macorís, where almost all Dominican rums are produced. Maturation takes place in oak barrels according to the solera system. The Oliver & Oliver company also makes other rums, such as Opthimus.

Name	Alc. %		🍃	🍍	🥃
Cubaney 3Y	38				🛡
Cubaney 5Y	38				🛡
Cubaney 8Y Solera Reserve	38				🛡
Cubaney Gran Reserva 18 Years Selecto	38				🛡
Cubaney Gran Reserva 21 Years Selecto	38				🛡
Cubaney Gran Reserve 25 Years Tesoro [T]	38				🛡
Cubaney Gran Reserve 30 Years Centenario	38				🛡

DICTADOR

ORIGIN

At the end of the eighteenth century, Severo Arango y Ferro settled in the region that we now know as Colombia. Because of his style and character he was soon given the nickname 'dictador'. He grew into one of the key figures in the trade of sugar cane spirits, which were also used as a means of payment at the time. In 1913, one of his descendants opened the Destilería Colombiana. Don Julio Arango y Parra spent his entire life keeping the myth of his ancestor and his passion for rum alive. But it was not until 2009 that this rum really made an international breakthrough.

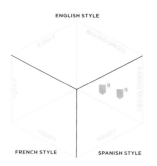

ENGLISH STYLE

FRENCH STYLE

SPANISH STYLE

The rums are made on the basis of virgin sugar honey, distilled partly in a copper pot still and partly in a steel column still. The distillate is then allowed to mature in used oak barrels and blended according to the solera system. The XO series is particularly interesting for connoisseurs: the Perpetual is made in the old copper still, whereas the Insolent comes from the more modern steel column still. The 100 series, on the other hand, is a rum that comes from the column still, after which it is left to mature for a hundred months.

Name	Alc. %				
Dictador 100 Claro [18]	40				🔵
Dictador 100 Amber	40				🔵
Dictador 100 Coffee	40				🔵
Dictador 100 Orange	40				🔵
Dictador 12 Years Solera [19]	40				🔵
Dictador 20 Years	40				🔵
Dictador XO Insolent	40				🔵
Dictador XO Perpetual	40				🔵

DIPLOMÁTICO

ORIGIN

The distillery that produces Ron Diplomático today has existed since 1959. However, it was largely owned by the beverage giant Seagram's until the beginning of the twenty-first century. At the end of 2002 everything was put up for sale and it was purchased by Venezuelan entrepreneurs who expanded the company, turning it into the international brand that we know today.

The portrait on the label shows Don Juancho Nieto Meléndez, a rum collector who lived in the region at the end of the nineteenth century. The brand name Diplomático had already been patented in several countries, and the owners therefore had to find a substitute name. Botucal was the name of one of the plantations that provided the sugar cane and this was chosen as an alternative. So if you see a bottle of Botucal, you now know it is the same as a bottle of Diplomático.

ENGLISH STYLE

FUNKY

BAKING SPICES

FUNKY

BAKING SPICES

20

FRUITY

FRUITY

FRENCH STYLE

SPANISH STYLE

The modern distillery is located at the foot of the Andes, near the sugar cane plantations, and it has a natural spring. The production is highly diverse. The company uses various types of stills and works with both molasses and virgin cane honey. Maturation mainly takes place in used Scotch whisky barrels and bourbon barrels. Sherry barrels (Oloroso and Pedro Ximénez) are also used for the Vintage and the Ambassador.

Name	Alc. %				
Diplomático Blanco Reserva	40				
Diplomático Añejo	40				
Diplomático 8 Years Reserva	40				
Diplomático Reserva Exclusiva 12 Years [20]	40				
Diplomático Ambassador	47				
Diplomático Vintage 2001 Limited	43				

DON PAPA

ORIGIN

Ron Don Papa derives its name from the story of Dionisio Magbuelas, one of the heroes of the Philippine Revolution. He is known to the indigenous population as Papa Isio: a shaman, healer, rebel and visionary. The brand was created in 2011 and marketed for the first time in 2012.

FLAVOUR AND AROMA

Not much is known about the production. The standard Don Papa is said to contain seven-year-old rum, whereas the Don Papa 10Y, which was launched in 2015, contains blends that are older than ten years. However, independent tests have shown high levels of added vanilla and glycerol, as a result of which the rum looks much older than it actually is. No vanilla was found in the Don Papa 10Y, but it had abnormally high levels of glycerol.

Name	Alc. %				
Don Papa	40				
Don Papa 10Y	43				

 # DON Q

ORIGIN

Around 1820, a Spaniard by the name of Juan Sebastian Serrallés arrived in Ponce, Puerto Rico, where he started both a sugar cane plantation and a family. In 1865, his son Don Juan became the first in the family to produce rum, using a copper still that he had bought in France.

The Don Q label, inspired by Don Quixote, was launched in 1934, immediately after the repeal of the US Prohibition Act. The rum was very successful and the distillery acquired column stills a year later.

FLAVOUR AND AROMA

The aim is to create the softest rum possible, a rum that is accessible to everyone. Ramon Marrero used Don Q to create the first piña colada in 1954. However, their showpiece is Gran Añejo, a blend of rums that range between nine and fifty years.

Name	Alc. %	🗄	🌿	🍍	🍾
Don Q Cristal	40				🔵
Don Q Gold	40				🔵
Don Q Añejo	40				🔵
Don Q 151 (overproof)	75.5				🔵
Don Q Gran Añejo	40				🔵

FACUNDO

ORIGIN

Bacardi has tried to boost its image in recent years. Besides purchasing other brands, it also focuses on a premium line of its own, named after its founder Don Facundo Bacardí.

FLAVOUR AND AROMA

This range comprises four products: Facundo Neo is a blend of rums up to eight years old that are passed through a charcoal filter. What makes Facundo Eximo so special is that it is blended before its ten-year maturation rather than after. Facundo Exquisito is a blend of rums between seven and twenty-three years old. The blend is then finished in sherry barrels for a month. The showpiece of the range is Facundo Paraiso, a blend of rums up to twenty-three years old from Bacardi's family reserve, matured in used, French oak barrels.

Name	Alc. %	🛢	🌿	🍍	🍶
Facundo Neo	40				🔻
Facundo Eximo	40				🔻
Facundo Exquisito	40				🔻
Facundo Paraiso	40				🔻

FLOR DE CAÑA

ORIGIN

Flor de Caña, which is Spanish for the sugar cane flower, comes from the town of Chichigalpa in Nicaragua. The brand name has existed since 1937 and has always been owned by the Pellas family. It is one of the market leaders in Central America.

However, the brand has received some heavy criticism in recent years. It was noted that after their bottles were restyled in 2014, they no longer indicated the 'Years'. Although the bottles previously said '4 Years', since 2014 they have only shown a '4'. This suggests that the age no longer refers to the youngest rum in the blend and that the bottle contains even younger rums.

In 2015, the brand received unwelcome attention once again when reports revealed the miserable state of the health and working conditions of its workers. A lot of rum bars dumped their stock of Flor de Caña as a form of protest and posted photos of the action in the social media.

FLAVOUR AND AROMA

The distillery uses the classic work method for this style of rum: molasses as the basis, distilled in column stills and matured in oak barrels.

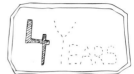

Name	Alc. %				
Flor de Caña Extra Seco 4	40				▾
Flor de Caña Extra Lite 4	40				▾
Flor de Caña Añejo Oro	40				▾
Flor de Caña Añejo Clasico	40				▾
Flor de Caña Blanco Reserva 7	40				▾
Flor de Caña Gran Reserva 7	40				▾
Flor de Caña Gran Reserva 90 Proof	40				▾
Flor de Caña Centenario 12	40				▾
Flor de Caña Centenario 18	40				▾
Flor de Caña Centenario 25	40				▾

SP HAVANA CLUB

ORIGIN

Havana Club was launched in 1934 as the rum brand of the Arechabala family, that founded a distillery in Cárdenas in 1878. The distillery was nationalised after the Cuban Revolution and the family fled to Spain and the United States. But Havana Club continued to exist and half of it is currently owned by beverage giant Pernod Ricard; the other half is state-owned. The rum could not be sold in the United States because of the trade embargo. However, the Arechabalas' recipe was bought by Bacardi, which has marketed the rum in the United States under the name of Havana Club since 1994.

ENGLISH STYLE

FUNKY   BAKING SPICES

SUGARY   BAKING SPICES

24

25

FRUITY   FRUITY

FRENCH STYLE   SPANISH STYLE

All their rums are molasses-based, distilled in column stills and matured in oak barrels. The age stated on the bottle is the age of the youngest rum. Only 1,000 bottles of the showpiece Máximo are produced each year.

Name	Alc. %	🛢	🌿	🍍	🍶
Havana Club 3Y [24]	40				
Havana Club 5Y Añejo Especial	40				
Havana Club 7Y	40				
Havana Club Ritual Cubano	37.5				
Havana Club Selección de Maestros [25]	45				
Havana Club 15Y	40				
Havana Club Máximo	40				
Havana Club Unión	40				

INGENIO MANACAS

ORIGIN

In 1948, the Spanish merchant Sánchez Romate sent his right-hand man Juan Jiménez Villalba to Cuba to see whether his brandy and sherry were selling well there. Villalba discovered that the barrels that were used there were perfect for maturing Cuban rum. One of the local distillers who traded rum with Villalba was Ingenio Manacas, hence the rum's name.

After the Cuban Revolution, Villalba managed to smuggle some of his barrels to Jerez. He used them to extend the solera system, which is still being used to this very day.

FLAVOUR AND AROMA

Ingenio Manacas Extra Añejo is a unique blend of various Caribbean rums from the Dominican Republic, Panama and Venezuela. The rum types are of different ages, which makes the story even more complex. The rum from the Dominican Republic is five years old, those from Panama and Venezuela are four years old. Ingenio Manacas Extra Añejo is matured for three years more in Jerez de la Frontera, in the south of Spain.

All barrels to which the solera system is applied are used amontillado sherry barrels. They give the rum a superb complexity.

Name	Alc. %				
Ingenio Manacas Extra Añejo	38	■			■

LEGENDARIO

ORIGIN

Hardly anything can be found about the origin of this brand. According to the earliest listing, since 1878 this rum has been made in the city of Cárdenas, where the Havana Club was produced at the time. Other sources claim that the rum has been made at the Bocoy distillery since 1946. We know for certain that the brand is still active, and its production is probably being continued elsewhere.

FLAVOUR AND AROMA

The Elixir de Cuba roughly tries to be to rum what Drambuie (a liqueur based on Scotch) is to whisky. In this case, two to four-year-old rum is blended with raisin extracts and diluted with demineralised water.

Name	Alc. %	🛢	🌿	🍍	🍶
Legendario Añejo Blanco	40				🛡
Legendario Dorado	38				🛡
Legendario Elixir de Cuba	34				🛡
Legendario Añejo 9Y	40				🛡
Legendario Añejo 15Y	40				🛡

PANAMA

MALECON

ORIGIN

Malecon is produced by Caribbean Spirits Inc. in Panama, but it is made according to a recipe that was brought from Cuba by a refugee.

FLAVOUR AND AROMA

Its flavour profile is in line with other Cuban rums. The rum is made from molasses, distilled in a column still and matured in oak barrels.

Name	Alc. %	🛢	🌿	🍍	🍶
Malecon 3 Years	40				🍶
Malecon 12 Years	40				🍶
Malecon 15 Years Reserva Superior	40				🍶
Malecon 18 Years Reserva Imperial	40				🍶
Malecon 21 Years Reserva Imperial	40				🍶
Malecon 25 Years Reserva Imperial	40				🍶
Malecon 1979 Esplendida	40				🍶
Malecon 1976 Esplendida	40				🍶

MATUSALEM

ORIGIN

The Alvarez family, like many other rum producers, fled the country during the Cuban Revolution. A lot of them chose the Dominican Republic, because its climate and soil were very similar to Cuba and therefore perfectly suited for restarting production.

FLAVOUR AND AROMA

The Alvarez family currently do not have a distillery of their own, but have instead signed a long-term contract with a company in Santiago for distilling their rum. The rum is matured in oak barrels according to the solera system.

Name	Alc. %	🛢	🌿	🍍	🍶
Matusalem Platino	40				�
Matusalem Extra Añejo	40				▮
Matusalem Solera 7 Years	40				▮
Matusalem Clásico 10 Years	40				▮
Matusalem Gran Reserva 15 Years	40				▮
Matusalem Gran Reserva 18 Years	40				▮
Matusalem Gran Reserva Solera 23 Years	40				▮

MILLONARIO

ORIGIN

In 1904, a sugar factory, where a local farmers' cooperative processed sugar on a small scale, was set up in Chiclayo, a little village in the north of Peru. The small sugar factory was bought eighteen years later by Don Rolando Piera de Castillo, a landowner. Due to the lack of know-how, he sent his eldest son Augusto to Cambridge University to study chemistry. The latter returned in the summer of 1938, not only with a degree but also with a mill and a Scottish column still. The brand name Millonario was launched in 1950. Since the production of rum is very labour-intensive, and not many people could afford the product, it was named 'Por los millonarios'.

When Fabio Rossi, the son of a beverage importer and the founder of Rum Nation, was searching for new products in 2004 in Peru, he was introduced to the Millonario and decided to launch the brand internationally.

FLAVOUR AND AROMA

As the name suggests, maturation of the 15 Years Solera takes place in oak barrels according to the solera system. The XO, on the other hand, is a blend of rums up to twenty years old.

Name	Alc. %				
Millonario 15 Years Sistema Solera	40				
Millonario XO [28]	40				

 MOCAMBO

ORIGIN

Mocambo is a brand made by the Mexican beverage producer Licores Veracruz. This producer had been in business since the end of the nineteenth century, but was purchased in 1950 and moved to the city of Córdoba by its current owners, the Villanueva Barragán family. In addition to rum, it also makes tequila, mezcal and other spirits.

FLAVOUR AND AROMA

The basis of the rum is fermented molasses, distilled in column stills. Maturation takes place in used bourbon and whisky barrels. The bottle of the Mocambo 20 Years is very distinctive because of its bark cover, which was designed by the Mexican artist Victor Fernández.

Name	Alc. %				
Mocambo 10 Years	40				
Mocambo 15 Years 40%	40				
Mocambo 20 Years 40%	40				

RON *palma*
ULATA
de CUBA

SP MULATA

ORIGIN

This Cuban rum is from Heriberto Duquesne, Villa Clara. The distillery is over fifty years old and is built on a 150-year-old tradition. It produces three million litres a year, making it the third largest producer on the island.

FLAVOUR AND AROMA

The rum is produced from molasses and distilled in a column still. It has a light character and is matured in small, unused American oak barrels of 180 litres. The age stated on the bottle is the age of the youngest rum in the blend.

Name	Alc. %				
Mulata 5 Years Añejo	38				
Mulata 7 Years Gran Reserva	38				

VENEZUELA

SP OCUMARE

ORIGIN

Ocumare's first forays in the world of rum date back to 1938. Production started in Caracas, in a small company with just four employees and a small copper pot still.
In 1950, production was moved to Hacienda De Guadelupe in the little town of Ocumare de Tuy. It was there that a column still was used for the first time. The company can still be found at this address today, although it has become a hypermodern distillery. Master distiller and master blender Andres Colmenares makes sure that the rum still maintains the old traditions.

FLAVOUR AND AROMA

This molasses-based rum is matured in used bourbon barrels. Venezuelan law prescribes that rum should mature for at least two years, which is why the Blanco Especial is run through a charcoal filter after maturation to remove the excess colour.

Name	Alc. %	🛢	🌿	🍍	👅
Ocumare Blanco Especial	40				▢
Ocumare Añejo Especial 3 Years	40				▢
Ocumare Gold 12 Years	40				▢

PAMPERO

ORIGIN

Pampero was started in 1938 by Alejandro Hernández, a fisherman's son from Isla de Margarita. The brand is currently part of the larger Diageo Group and most of the production takes place in Ocumare.

FLAVOUR AND AROMA

The molasses-based rum is distilled in column stills. Maturation takes place in oak barrels. The rum was one of the first to be allowed by the Venezuelan government to use the 'añejo' label. Ages are no longer stated on the bottle today. Only after much detective work did we discover that the Pampero Aniversario, which is supplied in a leather cover, contains rums between two and eight years old.

Name	Alc. %	🛢	🌿	🍍	🍶
Pampero Blanco	37.5				🔻
Pampero Especial	40				🔻
Pampero Selección	40				🔻
Pampero Aniversario	40				🔻

RON VIEJO DE CALDAS

ORIGIN

This rum brand is produced by Industria Licorera de Caldas in Colombia, at an altitude of 2,200 metres (7,200 ft) in the Andes.

FLAVOUR AND AROMA

The basis of this rum is sugar cane honey, which is distilled with pure mountain water from the springs at the Nevado del Ruiz. The rum is then laid down in oak barrels. Industria Licorera de Caldas has almost eighty years of experience to rely on and they market four types of rum today: Tradicional, Añejo 5 Años, Añejo 8 Años and Especial 15 Años.

Name	Alc. %	🛢	🌿	🍍	🍾
Ron Viejo de Caldas Tradicional	35				▼
Ron Viejo de Caldas Añejo 5 Años	35				▼
Ron Viejo de Caldas Añejo 8 Años	35				▼
Ron Viejo de Caldas Especial 15 Años	35				▼

SANTA TERESA

ORIGIN

Santa Teresa is one of the largest rum producers in the Caribbean and has produced super-premium rums for more than two centuries.

Fun fact: In addition to their love of rum, the owners and employees also share a passion for rugby and a rugby pitch was even constructed on the site. So you can have a game of rugby at Hacienda Santa Teresa next to a 100-year old pot still. The company is convinced that a good rugby match imposes the same requirements as making a good rum: teamwork, trust and fine performance.

FLAVOUR AND AROMA

The rums are matured at the Hacienda Santa Teresa site in American oak barrels and French limousin barrels, using the solera system. The passion that the makers put into their rum-making can be tasted in every bottle.

Today, Santa Teresa produces three rums: Claro, Gran Reserva and 1796. The last of these is undoubtedly the showpiece of the brand. It is an exceptional rum in all respects, with a rich flavour, a seductive smell and a deep colour. Santa Teresa Solera 1796 is deservedly considered to be one of the best rums in its price range and was awarded the very high score of 96 points by the *Wine Enthusiast*.

Name	Alc. %			
Santa Teresa Claro	40			
Santa Teresa Gran Reserva	40			
Santa Teresa 1796	40			

SANTIAGO DE CUBA

ORIGIN

Santiago de Cuba is a product of Corporación Cuba Ron, a distillery that also produces the well-known Havana Club brand. Santiago de Cuba was created in 1862 as *Ron Ligero* i.e. a light rum.

FLAVOUR AND AROMA

The rum is distilled in a continuous still according to the Cuban tradition and matured in oak barrels. According to Cuban super-stition, the nearby railway gives the rum its excep-tional flavour. The distillers claim that the vibrations of the passing trains create an exceptional maturation process. The entire process is strictly controlled by the *Maestri Roneri di Santiago di Cuba*, the guardians of the Cuban rum culture.

Name	Alc. %	🛢	🌿	🍍	🍾
Santiago De Cuba Carta Blanca	38				▮
Santiago De Cuba Añejo	38				▮
Santiago De Cuba Añejo Superior 11 Años	40				▮
Santiago De Cuba Extra Añejo 12 Años	40				▮
Santiago De Cuba Extra Añejo 20 Años	40				▮
Santiago De Cuba Extra Añejo 25 Años	40				▮

SP SUMMUM

ORIGIN

The rum arose from a cooperation between various connoisseurs of spirits, including the Cuban *maestro ronero* Juan Alberto Alvarez.

FLAVOUR AND AROMA

Summum sees itself as a Spanish-style rum, even though it is made from sugar cane juice. There are three variants that are all based on the same rum. This rum is blended using the solera system and its average age is twelve years. The difference between the three variants is in their finish. The Reserva Especial is not subject to any additional maturation, whereas the Whisky Cask and the Cognac Cask are given final maturation in Ben Nevis whisky barrels and Normandin-Mercier cognac barrels.

Name	Alc. %				
Summum Reserva Especial	38				🥃
Summum Whisky Cask	43				🥃
Summum Cognac Cask	43				🥃

PRODUCTO CUBANO

IMPORTADO

Ron Varadero

AÑEJO 15 AÑOS

à lo Cubano

GRAN RESERVA

ESTABLECIDOS EN 1862

Destilado y Embotellado por
Destilería Nauyú, Fundada en 1844
Ciego de Avila, Cuba

38% ALC. VOL. CUBA 70 cl e

VARADERO es marca registrada por Corporación CIMEX S.A
siendo la única autorizada para su exportación

VARADERO

ORIGIN

The Varadero of the Varadero Rum Distillery is distilled, matured and bottled in Santiago de Cuba. This distillery began business in 1862 and produced the first Cuban lightly matured rum. The south-eastern coastal area of Cuba is squeezed between the Atlantic Ocean and the Sierra Maestra, and has an ideal climate for growing the Media Luna sugar cane.

FLAVOUR AND AROMA

Cuba has a very rich rum history with a lot of variation and distinctive characterics for each brand. However, that diversity decreased enormously as a result of nationalisation under Castro. Varadero is a typical Cuban rum: very light, dry and natural.

Name	Alc. %				
Ron Varadero Silver Dry	40				▢
Ron Varadero Añejo	40				▢
Ron Varadero Añejo 3 Años	40				▢
Ron Varadero Añejo 5 Años	40				▢
Ron Varadero Añejo 7 Años	38				▢
Ron Varadero Añejo 15 Años	38				▢

ZACAPA

ORIGIN

Zacapa was distilled for the first time in 1976, when Licoreras de Guatemala decided to distil a special rum for the centenary celebrations of the village of Zacapa. Zacapa is produced with sugar cane that grows on the volcanic plateau in the southwest of Guatemala, around 350 metres (1,150 ft) above sea level.

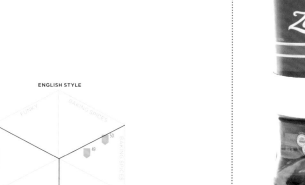

ENGLISH STYLE

FRENCH STYLE | SPANISH STYLE

FLAVOUR AND AROMA

Sugar cane honey from the first pressing of the sugar cane is used as the basis. This creates a soft, round and slightly sweet flavour in the rum. Zacapa is a blend of various rums with ages ranging from six to 25 years. Those rums were then matured in American whiskey barrels, Spanish sherry barrels and Pedro Ximénez barrels according to the solera system. Zacapa is always matured in the thin mountain air at an altitude of 2,300 metres (7,500 ft), in The House Above the Clouds. The low temperature slows down the maturation process, while the low atmospheric pressure and thin air encourage the absorption of the flavours of the wood. This slow maturation creates a rum with an extraordinary aroma and a soft flavour.

Name	Alc. %				
Zacapa 15 Years	40				
Zacapa Centenario 23 Years [49]	40				
Zacapa 23 Years Edicion Negra	40				
Zacapa Centenario XO [50]	40				
Zacapa Reserva Limitada 2013	45				

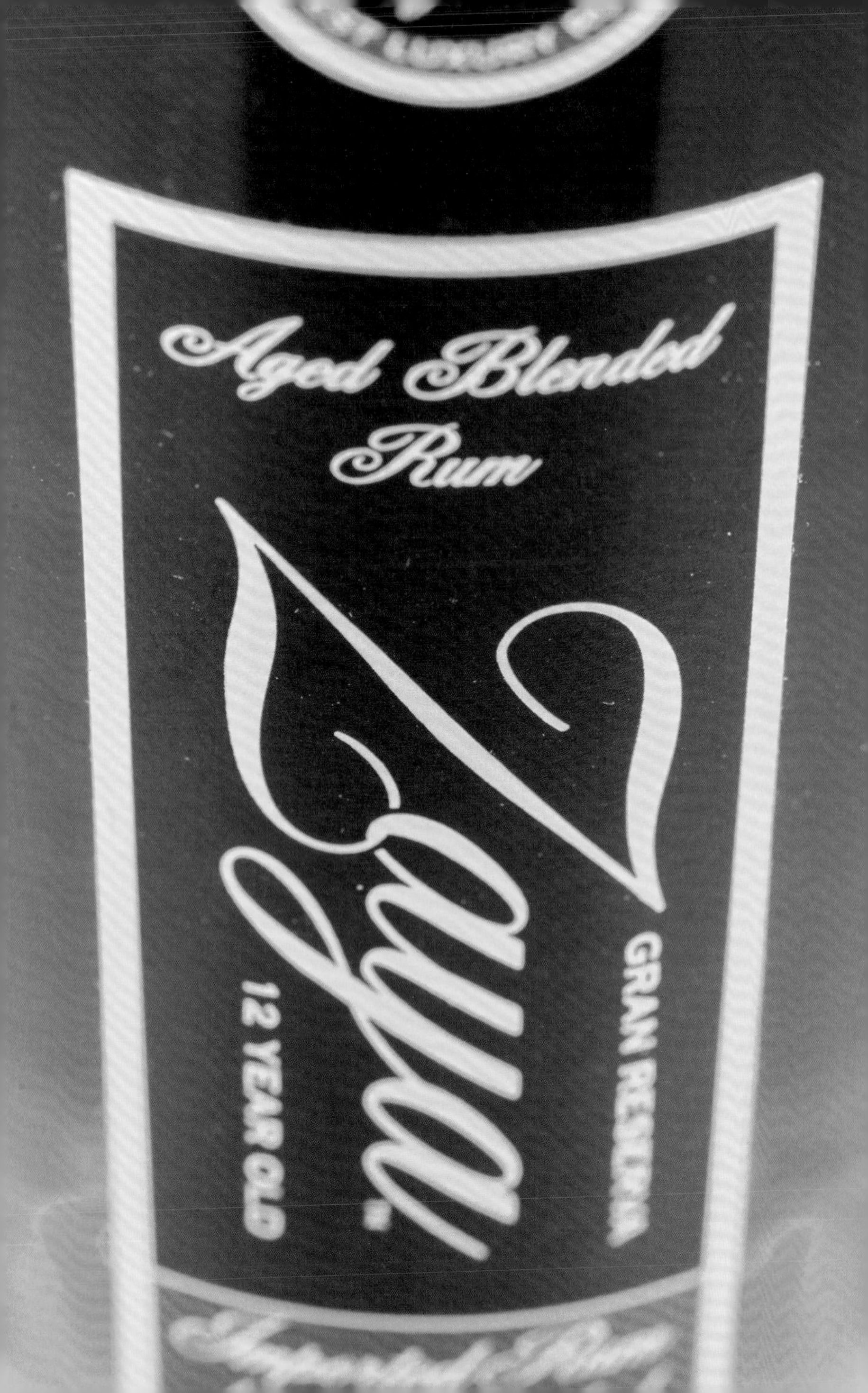
Aged Blended Rum
Zaya
GRAN RESERVA
12 YEAR OLD

ZAYA

ORIGIN

Zaya was originally produced by Licoreras de Guatemala, the distillery of the well-known Zacapa brand. But Diageo took over the worldwide distribution from Licoreras de Guatemala in 2008 and it preferred Zacapa. Zaya was forced to look for a new distillery and finally found one in the Angostura Distillery in Trinidad.

FLAVOUR AND AROMA

Both the variant from Guatemala and the one from Trinidad are available. You will, of course, need to put a little more effort into obtaining an original bottle from Guatemala. Zaya Gran Reserva 12 Years is made of a blend of three to five rums that have matured in bourbon and whisky barrels for at least twelve years.

Name	Alc. %				
Zaya Gran Reserva 12 Years	40				

OUTSIDERS

Outsiders are rums that cannot be classified under a single heading. They are a bit 'out of the box' or a combination of various styles. Independent bottlers, who select barrels of rum at various distilleries and let them mature further if necessary to create a rum of their own, are also considered outsiders.

BANKS

ORIGIN

This rum is an ode to the eighteenth-century explorer and botanist Joseph Banks, who charted large parts of the Pacific Ocean together with Captain Cook. The brand was started in 2008 by Arnaud de Trabuc, a former CEO of the Angostura Group and director of Thomas Hine & Company. Bacardi purchased the brand in 2015.

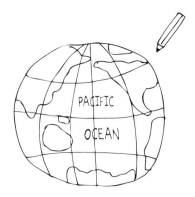

FLAVOUR AND AROMA

Banks tries to offer a complex end product by mixing various styles. Their two best-known rum variants are 5 Island and 7 Golden Age. 5 Island is a blend of twenty-one rums from six different distilleries and five different countries and regions: Jamaica, Trinidad, Guyana, Barbados and Java. 7 Golden Age is an amber rum based on a blend of twenty-three rums from eight distilleries and seven countries and regions: Jamaica, Trinidad, Guyana, Barbados, Panama, Guatemala and Java.

They occasionally launch a special edition or single cask. The Endeavour Limited Edition is a prime example. It is a blend of two rums that have matured for at least sixteen years and were selected from the exclusive 'reserves' of Banks. Only 1,743 bottles of this rum were produced.

Name	Alc. %	🍶	🌿	🍍	🍾
Banks 5 Island	43	▾			▾
Banks 7 Golden Age	43	▾			
Banks The Endeavour Limited Edition	43				▾

BERRY BROS. & RUDD

ORIGIN

Besides a good collection of rums, these wine and spirit merchants from London also have an entire bottling line of their own.

FLAVOUR AND AROMA

The creators visit various distilleries in all the rum-producing countries where they purchase barrels, after which they bottle the rums themselves. Their expertise always ensures good quality. But the flavour depends entirely on the style, the country and the bottle.

Name	Alc. %				
Berry's Grenada 13Y	46				▼
Berry's Panama 10Y	46				▼
Berry's Fijan 9Y	46				▼
Berry's Barbados 10Y	46				▼
Berry's Guadeloupe 12Y	46				▼

BLACKADDER

ORIGIN

Blackadder was started by Robin Tucek and John Lamond in 1995. Their distillery was named after the Scottish bishop John Blackadder. They have also translated their love for whisky into a book, *The Malt Whisky File*, a reference work that contains a list of all the available whiskies in the world.

FLAVOUR AND AROMA

Blackadder is an independent whisky bottler that believes that as few filtered spirits as possible should be used. This ensures that less of the original flavour will be lost, although it may make the contents of the bottle slightly cloudier. In addition to whisky, they also have a number of bottled rums that have been given very specific maturation. An example is the Blackadder Demerara 1992, which has matured in barrels that previously held a peated Islay whisky. The alcohol percentages of these rums are mostly fairly high too.

Name	Alc. %				
Blackadder Panama 2000 12Y	57.3				🍶
Blackadder Demerara 1992 9Y (Islay Cask)	46				🍶
Blackadder St. Lucia 1999 12Y	68.2				🍶
Blackadder Fiji 2001 11Y	63.9				🍶

BLUE BAY

ORIGIN

Blue Bay is a Mauritian rum made at the Medine Distillery in Bambous, which started up in 1911. This distillery is part of a group that also specialises in property, agriculture and tourism.

FLAVOUR AND AROMA

Blue Bay is a mixture of 70%-80% sugar cane-based rum and 20%-30% molasses-based rum. The company only uses unmatured white rum. It is very sharp and mainly has vegetal and fruity tones.

Name	Alc. %				
Blue Bay White	40				

BONPLAND

SB

CRAFTED
IN THE NEW WORLD

DOUBLE AGED IN GERMAN
RED WINE

RUM

MOSEL ✦ GERMANY

ROUGE

 BONPLAND

ORIGIN

The makers of Ferdinand's Gin from the Moselle region in Germany have recently started focusing on rum as well. What makes this rum unique is the second stage of maturation, which takes place in casks that were previously used for maturing German wine.

The name Bonpland is a reference to Alexander von Humboldt's travelling companion Aimé Bonpland, whose notes during their travels made a huge contribution to science.

FLAVOUR AND AROMA

Bonpland Blanc is a blend of various rums from Trinidad, Jamaica, Guyana, Indonesia, the French West Indies and Barbados. After the first maturation, the blend is topped up with a small amount of rum from the French Antilles and Batavia Arrack from Java. The second maturation is in Chardonnay casks from VDP Weingut Bernhard Huber in Baden.

Bonpland Rouge VSOP is a blend of rums from Trinidad, Jamaica, Guyana, Guatemala and Nicaragua. The second maturation takes place in Pinot Noir casks from VDP Weingut Friedrich Becker.

Name	Alc. %				
Bonpland Blanc	40	▼			▼
Bonpland Rouge VSOP	40	▼			▼

CADENHEAD

ORIGIN

Cadenhead is the oldest existing independent bottler of Scotch whisky, but their range also contains some excellent rums. In contrast to many others, they do not add anything to the products and do not use a chill filter either, as this eliminates much of the original flavour.

FLAVOUR AND AROMA

All the variants come from hand-picked barrels and are therefore only available as limited editions. The company sometimes also plays with finishes by using old barrels, such as a cask that was used to store Laphroaig (a heavily peated whisky).

Name	Alc. %	📦	🌿	🍍	🍾
Cadenhead Brazilian Green Label Rum 12Y/0	46				⬛
Cadenhead Cuban Green Label Rum 11Y/0	46				⬛
Cadenhead Cuban Green Label Rum 11Y/0	46				⬛
Cadenhead Nicaraguan Green Label Rum 8Y/0	46				⬛
Cadenhead Nicaraguan Green Label Rum 9Y/0	46				⬛
Cadenhead Barbados Green Label Rum 10Y/0	46				⬛
Cadenhead Barbados Blackrock 11Y/0	59.1				⬛
Cadenhead Demerara Green Label Rum 12Y/0	46				⬛
Cadenhead Demerara Green Label Rum 15Y/0	46				⬛
Cadenhead Demerara Green Label Rum 12Y/0 46% Finish: Laphroaig cask	46				⬛
Cadenhead Demerara Green Label Rum Distilled 1975	40.5				⬛
Cadenhead Demerara Uitvlugt 12Y/0	62				⬛
Cadenhead Demerara Enmore 18Y/0	63.3				⬛
Cadenhead Guyanan Green Label Rum 12Y/0	46				⬛
Cadenhead Jamaican Green Label Rum 10Y/0	46				⬛
Cadenhead Jamaican Green Label Rum 14Y/0	46				⬛
Cadenhead Jamaican Hampden 8Y/0	63.2				⬛
Cadenhead St. Lucia Green Label Rum 11Y/0	46				⬛
Cadenhead Trinidad Green Label Rum 11Y/0	46				⬛
Cadenhead Haitian Green Label Rum 5Y/0	46				⬛
Cadenhead Haitian Green Label Rum 7Y/0	46				⬛

COMPAGNIE DES INDES

ORIGIN

The idea behind Compagnie des Indes comes from the working method of the former Portuguese, Dutch, English and French trading companies that imported rare goods from far-away countries. The company bottles blends and single casks from various rum-producing countries.

FLAVOUR AND AROMA

Sugars, colorants or other additives are never used. You can also read on every bottle from the single casks which distillery the rum comes from and when it was bottled. This young company now produces more than fifty variants and a lot more are planned for the future!

Name	Alc. %	🛢	🌿	🍍	🍶
Compagnie des Indes Boulet de Canon N° 1	46	▮			▮
Compagnie des Indes Caraïbes	40	▮			▮
Compagnie des Indes Latino	40	▮			▮
Compagnie des Indes Barbados 16 ans 1998-2015 Cask #BD47	45				▮
Compagnie des Indes Belize 8 ans 2005-2014 Cask #SF48	64				▮
Compagnie des Indes Cuba 16 ans 1998-2014 Cask #CM5	45				▮
Compagnie des Indes Fiji 10 ans 2004-2015 Cask #SF13	44				▮
Compagnie des Indes Guadeloupe 16 ans 1998-2014 Cask #GM21	43				▮
Compagnie des Indes Guyana 24 ans 1990-2015 Cask #MEY04					▮
Compagnie des Indes Haiti 11 ans 2004-2015 Cask #BMH32 Cask strength	59.4				▮
Compagnie des Indes Indonesia 10 ans 2004-2015 Cask #SB22	43				▮
Compagnie des Indes Jamaica 14 ans 2000-2015 Cask #HP98	58				▮
Compagnie des Indes Martinique 13 ans 2002-2015 Cask #MA67	44				▮
Compagnie des Indes Panama 11 ans 2004-2015 Cask #MRS263	44				▮
Compagnie des Indes St. Lucia 13 ans 2002-2015 Cask #SLD46	56.3				▮
Compagnie des Indes Trinidad 24 ans 1991-2015 Cask #SC707	56.3				▮

COR COR

ORIGIN

On the tropical Japanese island of Minami Daito, the new Grace Rum distillery has been producing two top-quality rums since 2004, Cor Cor Green and Cor Cor Red.

FLAVOUR AND AROMA

Cor Cor Green is made from freshly pressed sugar cane juice and is distilled in traditional pot stills. These pot stills are also used for the Cor Cor Red, although that is based on molasses. Neither of the two rums is matured.

Name	Alc. %				
Cor Cor Green	40				🫗
Cor Cor Red	40				🫗

DUNCAN TAYLOR

ORIGIN

These independent bottlers are Scottish, from Glasgow to be precise. They started business in 1938 as barrel merchants. Duncan Taylor specialises in whisky in particular. Their warehouses are full of casks from distilleries that have closed down. Their offices have in the meantime moved from Glasgow to Huntly in Speyside and they now also create their own gin and rum.

FLAVOUR AND AROMA

This renowned independent bottler has managed to win various awards. It has a very wide range of single cask rums.

Name	Alc. %	🗄	🌿	🍍	🧴
Duncan Taylor St. Lucia 2002 11Y	52.6				🔻
Duncan Taylor South Pacific 200	54.8				🔻
Duncan Taylor Sancti Spiritus 1998 14Y	53.2				🔻
Duncan Taylor Caribbean rum 2001 11Y	46				🔻
Duncan Taylor Long Pond 2000 13Y	54.6				🔻
Duncan Taylor Monymusk 1997 15Y	53.4				🔻
Duncan Taylor Monymusk 2003 10Y	53.5				🔻
Duncan Taylor Dillon 2002 10Y	54.5				🔻
Duncan Taylor Bellevue 1998 14Y	52.3				🔻

DUNCAN TAYLOR
SINGLE CASK
Rum

ISTILLED IN: **FIJI**

DISTILLED IN

DZAMA

YLANG-
YLANG

PEPPER

CLOVES

VANILLA

ORIGIN

France lost some of its colonies that grew
sugar cane in the nineteenth century, so
the country had to look for an alternative.
That was found when Madagascar became a
French colony in 1896. In fact, under French
rule Madagascar became one of the world's
leaders in the production of sugar and vanilla.

Dzama was created by Lucien Fohine, a
wholesaler and distributor of whisky. He first
imported the rum in bottles, but he found
that it was cheaper to import it in barrels. He
needed a solution for all his empty whisky
barrels, which he found when he decided to
mature rum in them. The rum that he used
came from the small island of Nosy Be, in the
northwest of Madagascar, which is packed
with citrus trees and provides numerous indigenous spices, such as cloves, pepper, vanilla and ylang-ylang (an exotic flower). This
fantastic botanical bouquet gives the rum a
special character.

FLAVOUR AND AROMA

Molasses are used as the basis. Today, maturation largely takes place in used whisky barrels (mainly Chivas) and American oak barrels in which whisky and port have matured. The super-premium rums are matured in French limousin barrels. The whisky barrels for the Cuvée Blanche are washed with a citrus solution, which gives this rum a certain acidity and freshness.

Name	Alc. %				
Dzama Club Blanc 40%	40				
Dzama Cuvée Blanche Prestige 40%	40				
Dzama Cuvée Noire 40%	40				🛢
Dzama 3 Years 50%	50				🛢
Dzama 6 Years 40%	40				🛢
Dzama XV	40				🛢

LOST SPIRITS DISTILLERY

ORIGIN

Lost Spirits has its roots in the former Rational Spirits. It is a distillery in Charleston in the USA that focuses on rum. They use a special technological innovation, the famous THEA 1.0 reactor that considerably accelerates maturation.

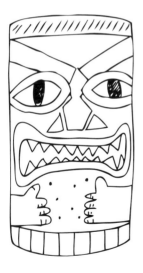

FLAVOUR AND AROMA

For the Santeria rum, they drew inspiration from legendary Caribbean black magic. The rum is based on an old Jamaican recipe that has been modernised. A lot of Jamaican rums use "dunder pits" to create an extra funky tone. For Santeria, the aim is to replicate this effect by selecting, cultivating and adding certain bacteria from dunder pits to the molasses.

The Navy Style and the Cuban Inspired 151 were launched recently, inspired by the English and Spanish styles, respectively.

For production they use molasses that are fermented slowly and naturally, after which distillation is carried out in a double pot still. No additives, colorants or sugars are added to it. Maturation is done in the THEA 1.0 reactor, which is claimed to achieve twenty years of maturation in six days. This may all sound unbelievable, but a lot of connoisseurs were absolutely astounded during blind tests and the creations by Lost Spirits were given amazingly high scores.

make this kind of rum requires a knowl of both technology and black magic.

Name	Alc. %	🍽	🌿	🍍	🍶
Santeria Rum	46				🔻
Navy Style	61				🔻
Cuban Inspired	75.5				🔻

ESTD 1941 THAILAND

Mekhong

THE SPIRIT
OF THAILAND

IMPORTED

Distilled Blended & Bottled by

BANGYIKHAN DISTILLERY

Product of Thailand

700ml e

35%vol.

MEKHONG

ORIGIN

Mekhong was the first golden spirit that was produced in Thailand. After it was launched in 1941, it soon became the most popular spirit, in part because of the border conflict with France about the Mekong river. That conflict was also the inspiration for the rum's name. The Bangyikhan Distillery, where this spirit is made, is located on the outskirts of the country's capital, Bangkok. In 2010, the brand was purchased by Sangsom, that stopped the original production. The brand has been relaunched recently, although now under an English label.

FLAVOUR AND AROMA

Although many people consider this spirit to be a whisky, we believe that it more resembles a rum. Some 95% of the distillate is made from sugar cane molasses; the remaining 5% comes from rice. The blend is then macerated with local herbs and spices.

Name	Alc. %				
Mekhong	35				

MEZAN

ORIGIN

Mezan is part of the Marussia Beverages group, which initially focused on the spirits trade between Western and Eastern Europe. It now has operations in thirty-one countries, including Belgium and the Netherlands.

FLAVOUR AND AROMA

Mezan acts as an independent bottler. Their cellar master travels the world looking for exceptional barrels of rum, which are allowed to mature further and are then bottled. None of the rums marketed by Mezan contain added sugars or colorants. The rums are also only slightly filtered so that each can retain its own character.

Name	Alc. %				
Mezan Panama 2006	40				🍾
Mezan Guyana Diamond 2003	40				🍾
Mezan Guyana Diamond 2005	40				🍾
Mezan Jamaica Long Pond 2000	40				🍾
Mezan Jamaica Worthy Park 2005	40				🍾
Mezan Jamaica XO	40				🍾

Distilled in Jamaica

MEZAN

EXTRA OLD RUM

❖

X.O
Jamaica

Aged at its very best, this rum has a pungent
nose with fresh banana and sweet spice and a
surprisingly light palate that shows complex
spice with hints of tobacco.

LOT Nº
022168

70cl   40% vol

· SINGLE DISTILLERY RUM ·
· MEZAN ·

OGASAWARA

ORIGIN

Around 1830, the local population of the Ogasawara Islands discovered that the climate was perfectly suited to growing sugar cane. They found a market eager for their products in the neighbouring Pacific Islands. Together with the fruit sector, the sugar cane sector is still big business there. The distillate of the local sugar cane is called 'Awazake' and it is very popular.

FLAVOUR AND AROMA

This molasses-based rum has been produced according to the traditional method at the Ogasawara Distillery since 1992. There are no matured variants of this rum so far. Compared to the Caribbean spirits, this rum has a more saline and spicier flavour.

Name	Alc. %				
Ogasawara	40				

OPTHIMUS

ORIGIN

Twenty years ago, the company Oliver y Oliver, which we also know from the Cubaney rum, decided to create a blend from the best distillates in the Caribbean. Rather than focusing on distilling, the *maestros roneros* or master rum makers visited all the distilleries to make their selections.

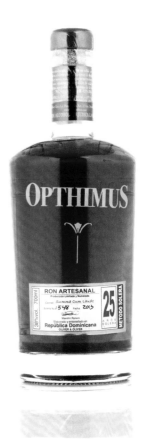

The blend consists of 96%-strength alcohol from the best distilleries in Panama, Guatemala, Nicaragua and the Dominican Republic. The blend is then mixed using 75% alcohol in the more aromatic French and English styles. This blend is matured in tempranillo barrels and bourbon barrels according to the solera system.

Originally, the warehouses in which the barrels were laid down were in San Francisco de Macoris, but they have now been moved to the Hato Nuevo Valley in a rural part of the Dominican capital, Santo Domingo. After the solera blend has been created, the two rums that have special finishes are matured for six months in malt whisky barrels or port barrels.

Name	Alc. %	🛢	🌿	🍍	🍶
Opthimus 15 Years	40	▮			▮
Opthimus 18 Years	40	▮			▮
Opthimus 21 Years	40	▮			▮
Opthimus 25 Years	40	▮			▮
Opthimus 25 Years malt whisky finish	43	▮			▮
Opthimus 25 Years port finish	43	▮			▮

PLANTATION

ORIGIN

The French cognac house Maison Ferrand has always maintained a close relationship with various distilleries in the Caribbean, because they sold their used cognac barrels to them. During one of these deals, Alexandre Gabriël, the master blender, was given the opportunity to taste some old samples from the private cellars of the rum producers. In the end, Maison Ferrand decided to buy these barrels and to launch them under the collective brand name Plantation.

The brand admits others too, so unique barrels can be bought through them. Some examples are the single casks chosen by the London tiki bar Trailer Happiness and the Limburg drinks importer The Nectar.

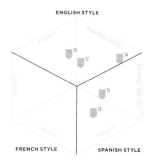

FLAVOUR AND AROMA

Plantation currently has products from various countries, but it also produces various blends. The Plantation 3 Stars is a white rum, a blend of rums from Barbados, Trinidad and Jamaica. The Original Dark, on the other hand, is a dark rum that consists of rums from Trinidad and Jamaica.

Name	Alc. %	🛢	🌿	🍍	🧴
Plantation 3 stars White	41.2	▮			▮
Plantation Original Dark [37]	40	▮			▮
Plantation Original Dark Overproof	73	▮			▮
Plantation Guatemala Gran Añejo [35]	42				▮
Plantation Guatemala XO	42				▮
Plantation Nicaragua 2003	42				▮
Plantation Panama 2004 [38]	42				▮
Plantation Jamaica 2001 [36]	42				▮
Plantation Trinidad 2001	42				▮
Plantation Barbados Gran Reserve 5 Years	40				▮
Plantation Barbados 2001	42				▮
Plantation Barbados XO 20th Anniv. [34]	40				▮
Plantation Guyana 2005	45				▮
Plantation St. Lucia 2004	43				▮
Plantation Stiggins' Fancy Pineapple rum	40	▮		▮	

RENEGADE
RUM COMP

ANY
RE ESSENTIAL
RIBBEAN.

RENEGADE
RUM COMP
SMALL-BATCH, ARTIS
NATURAL RUMS FROM
DISTILLERIES OF THE

1999

AGED 10 YEARS IN OAK CASKS

RENEGADE
RUM
COMPANY

ESSENTIAL CARIBBEAN COLLECTION

RENEGADE RUM

ORIGIN

One of the best-known Islay whisky producers, Bruichladdich, has also bottled a sturdy selection of rums besides its excellent line-up of single malts.

FLAVOUR AND AROMA

The rums have been selected from various distilleries and are always matured in a certain type of wine cask.

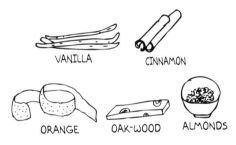

VANILLA   CINNAMON

ORANGE   OAK-WOOD   ALMONDS

Name	Alc. %	🛢	🌿	🍍	🍾
Renegade Four Square 6 Years Banyuls Cask (Barbados)	46				🬀
Renegade Epris 1999 10 Years Chât. Lafite (Brazil)	46				🬀
Renegade Paraiso 1996 12 Years Amarone Casks (Cuba)	46				🬀
Renegade Westerhall 1996 12 Years Chât. Margaux Casks (Grenada)	46				🬀
Renegade Gardel 1996 11 Years Chât. Latour Casks (Guadeloupe)	46				🬀
Renegade St. Lucia 1999 10 Years Chât. Lafleur Casks (St. Lucia)	46				🬀
Renegade Angostura 1991 17 Years Chât. LePin Casks (Trinidad)	46				🬀

RON DE JEREMY

ORIGIN

What started as a stunt by a couple of friends, developed into a high-quality product. The Finns at the One Eyed Spirits company believed that the drinks sector took itself too seriously, and decided to launch a rum based on the porn star Ron Jeremy. That choice was obvious, because Ron means 'rum'. The slogan of the rum therefore is particularly relevant: 'The rum for adults'.

FLAVOUR AND AROMA

Ron de Jeremy is made by Francisco 'Don Pancho' Fernandez, a master distiller and former Minister of Cuban Rum. You can therefore say that the rum is distilled by one of the most experienced and renowned master distillers, as well as being very accessible. The harmonious bouquet of vanilla and herbs blends in very nicely with the pleasant woody tones. The rum, which is matured in Panama in used bourbon barrels, is a blend of rums from Guyana, Barbados, Jamaica and Trinidad. So far, there is no variant with an alcohol content of 69%, which is perhaps surprising.

Name	Alc. %	🛢	🌿	🍍	🍶
Ron de Jeremy Reserva ⁴¹	40	▮			▮
Ron de Jeremy XO	40	▮			▮
Ron de Jeremy Spiced	38	▮	▮		▮
Ron de Jeremy Spiced, The Hardcore Edition	47	▮	▮		▮

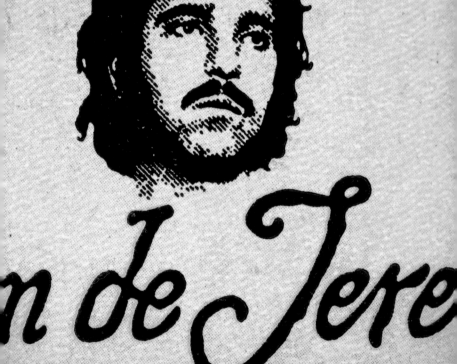

n de Jere

RESERVA

= the original adult =

RUM NATION

ORIGIN

Fabio Rossi literally grew up among the bottles. His father was a beverage importer and was the first to bring in Laphroaig and Barbancourt, names that are now well-known. When Fabio visited various distilleries in Scotland at the start of the 1990s, he noticed that their warehouses often contained barrels of rum. Those rums from Jamaica and Guyana were maturing there, next to single malt whiskies, so that they could be used in navy rums later. After Fabio had tasted this rum and been absolutely enchanted by the spirit, he asked Silvano Samaroli, another whisky bottler and a big name in the Italian drinks sector, for advice. Silvano taught Fabio about the differences between the styles and countries. Fabio later started purchasing rum barrels. The rest is history. Rum Nation was created in 1999.

ENGLISH STYLE

FRENCH STYLE

SPANISH STYLE

FLAVOUR AND AROMA

Although Fabio Rossi initially purchased English-style rum in particular, he also discovered the other styles during one of his journeys in the Caribbean. One of these styles is the Peruvian rum Millonario, which he relaunched as a separate product alongside the Rum Nation series. In addition to rums in the Spanish and the English styles, Fabio Rossi also has barrels from Martinique. Reimonenq, a rum from Guadeloupe, is handled the same way as Millonario and will continue to be marketed as a separate brand in addition to the Rum Nation series.

Name	Alc. %	🍾	🌿	🍍	🫙
Rum Nation Barbados 10Y	40				🫙
Rum Nation Barbados 12Y Anniversary	40				🫙
Rum Nation Caroni 1998-2014	55				🫙
Rum Nation Caroni 1999-2015	55				🫙
Rum Nation Demerara 23 Years 1990	45				🫙
Rum Nation Demerara 25 Years 1990	45				🫙
Rum Nation Demerara Solera no. 14	40				🫙
Rum Nation Jamaica White Pot Still	57				
Rum Nation Jamaica 8Y Pot Still	50				🫙
Rum Nation Jamaica 23Y Supreme Lord	45				🫙
Rum Nation Martinique Hors d'Âge (released 2014)	43				🫙
Rum Nation Panama 18 Years	40				🫙
Rum Nation Panama 18 Years Solera	40				🫙
Rum Nation Panama 21 Years	40				🫙
Rum Nation Peruano 8 Years [42]	42				🫙

SAILOR JERRY

ORIGIN

The rum is named after an exceptional man. Norman Keith Collins, also known as Sailor Jerry, was a founding father of old-school tattoos and was known for tattooing sailors. The rum is composed each year by a team of master blenders from William Grant & Sons who travel to the Caribbean to select the finest rums there. The result is a no-nonsense rum with aromas such as vanilla, cinnamon and nutmeg.

FLAVOUR AND AROMA

The recipe for Sailor Jerry Spiced Rum is based on the spices that were used to aromatise the rum on board sailing ships. The typical tones of vanilla and cinnamon can therefore be found in abundance in this spicy rum.

CINNAMON

VANILLA

Name	Alc. %	🛢	🌿	🍍	🧴
Sailor Jerry Spiced Rum	40	▮	▮		

SHACK

ORIGIN

Shack rum was launched in 2015 by Serge Buss, who had also marketed some top gins through Buss Spirits. This rum is inspired by the voodoo culture and is available in two variants, Shack Gold and Shack Spiced.

FLAVOUR AND AROMA

Shack Gold is a premium amber blended rum. Shack Spiced on the other hand is spiced with all kinds of secret herbs and spices. The production process is largely a secret, but is said to be based on an old Haitian recipe.

Name	Alc. %	🛢	🌿	🍍	🍾
Shack Gold	40	🔻			🔻
Shack Spiced 40%	40	🔻	🔻		🔻

ORIGINAL

AUSTRIA
INLÄNDER RUM

STROH

80

Sebastian Stroh

STROH

1832

The Spirit of Austria

 **STROH**

ORIGIN

Stroh is an *Inländer Rum*, a spirit that is popular in Austria, Hungary and Germany, and has a characteristic, soft and sweet flavour. It was originally marketed as a substitute for rum from tropical countries. Stroh was made for the first time in 1832 in Klagenfurt, and it is named after its creator Sebastian Stroh. Stroh is the best-known alcohol brand from Austria, and it is available in more than thirty countries.

FLAVOUR AND AROMA

Stroh is made from molasses that are distilled in a column still and to which all kinds of colorants, fragrances and flavourings have been added. *Inländer Rum* has aromas and flavours of vanilla, oak and a touch of orange and almond. The stronger variants are often used as ingredients for cocktails.

Name	Alc. %	🛢	🌿	🍍	🧴
Stroh 80	80		🔹	🔹	
Stroh 60	60		🔹	🔹	
Stroh 40	40		🔹	🔹	
Stroh 38	38		🔹	🔹	

WORLD'S END RUM

ORIGIN

2240 Spirits, the company behind World's End Rum, started in 2014 as the brainchild of Lester Schutters. What began as a particularly engrossing hobby rapidly grew into a success, allowing Lester to devote all his time to it and live his passion for rum. He focused on the spiced rum niche market, which had up to that point been dominated by the larger industrial players with products of corresponding industrial quality.

Name	Alc. %	🛢	🌿	🍍	🍶
World's End Dark Spiced	40	▾	▾		▾
World's End Tiki Spiced	40	▾	▾		▾

FLAVOUR AND AROMA

The Dark Spiced, which has been on the market since April 2015, is a blend of different styles with additional flavours from cocoa and oranges. This spiced rum immediately won various awards and has become renowned for its complexity.

World's End Tiki Spiced arose from a collaboration with one of the authors of this book, Tom Neijens. They looked for inspiration in the flavour patterns of tiki cocktails, more specifically the Navy Grog cocktail, which combines various dominant rums and herbs. The rum is a blend containing predominantly English-style rums, with additional flavours of cinnamon and allspice.

In addition to the rums, they also market a Falernum, a liqueur based on rum that is principally used for spicing up exotic cocktails.

START TO
RUM

People often ask us which rums they should start with, given the wide choice. Our answer is simple: Buy yourself a matured and a non-matured bottle of rum of each style, white and brown. Discovering the brand you prefer may be a bit of a quest, but it is an enjoyable quest nonetheless! Go out and see, taste and discover. Find inspiration in this book, visit the better rum or tiki bars or start tasting at home with a couple of friends.

HOW DO YOU DRINK RUM?

The way you prefer to drink rum is entirely up to you. Some prefer their rum straight, others go for a well-served cocktail or a delicious punch. Rum can suit any occasion: drink it in a refreshing cocktail on a sunny day, at a dinner with friends or as one for the road to conclude a pleasant evening. The spirit can be creative and stimulate your taste buds in various ways. Rum is a blank canvas, as it were, on which masterpieces can be created, with the artist as the sole consumer. We will limit ourselves to providing the brushes.

NEAT

Some rums are too good to mix. Super-premium rums simply prefer to stand alone. As with single malt whiskies, drinking rum straight sometimes causes heated discussions. Ice or no ice, a few drops of water or not... Not to mention the type of glass that is most appropriate. Actually, we can be fairly brief about this: There is no right or wrong way! You alone determine the way that you prefer to drink your rum, as long as you enjoy it. Besides, there's nothing preventing you from trying various ways until you have found what suits you. Moreover, your preference may also often depend on the type of rum, the occasion or even the company.

Our tip!
Drink rum at room temperature, without ice. Pour 3 to 6 cl (3 cl is sufficient to taste) into a small whisky tumbler or cognac glass, and let yourself be transported by the carousel of flavours. And maybe you'll only want to drink your rum that way from that moment on.

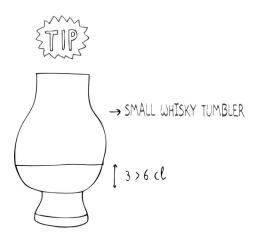

→ SMALL WHISKY TUMBLER

3 > 6 cl

TASTING RUM FOR THE FIRST TIME

Tasting rum for the first time is largely about having respect for the spirit. In other words: do not drain your glass in one go, but handle rum as if it were your lover. Study its colour, smell it and take a sip. You should preferably use a tulip-shaped glass with a wide bottom and a narrow top, also known as a snifter. The shape of the glass will help to better channel the aromas to your nose.

Pour about 3 cl of rum at room temperature into the glass. Warmth helps release the aromas so you can also hold the glass in your hands. If possible, put the glass in the palm of your hand and rotate it gently. This means that air will not get into your rum and change its texture. This technique will also disperse the aromas throughout the entire glassful and reduce the overpowering scent of alcohol when you smell the drink. Rum is therefore not swirled like wine.

When smelling rum, it is important to handle the contents of the glass gently. Do not stick your nose right into the glass, but keep a slight distance. Rum has a high alcohol content that can prevent you from sniffing the aromas if you stick your nose into the glass too deeply. Let your nose get used to the scent and then take a first sip. Roll the rum around in your mouth so you can catch its elementary flavour and let it rest on your tongue, after which you can roll it around your mouth once again. The greatest enjoyment comes afterwards, when you breathe out again after swallowing. A premium rum will endlessly pamper your taste buds after this first exhalation. But you must remember one thing: tasting is very subjective. The

SNIFFER

range of flavours and aromas in a rum will be different for everyone.

WITH WATER

Adding a few drops of water to your rum will slightly change the composition and release more flavours and aromas. You should of course use water that contains as few chemical additives as possible. Soft tap water is perfectly good for this. We would recommend that you start with just a drop of water and repeat until you have found the right balance.

WITH ICE

Adding ice can give your rum a fresh taste, and you may prefer to drink your rum slightly colder. There is nothing wrong with that, but do not use too much ice. Cold will numb the tastebuds and melted ice water is disastrous for the rum.

If you decide that you prefer your rum cool, choose ice that cannot melt in the glass. You can find all kinds of cooling cubes and pebble ice on the market.

AS A COCKTAIL

FIVE CLASSICS

The genuine classic rum cocktails are still popular guests at numerous tropical parties. They bring freshness during a hot summer night and undeniably remind you of exotic destinations. Appropriately, most rum cocktails were created in Cuba. Rum cocktails are also popular on cooler days. Simply replacing the rum with a dark variant gives the cocktail more depth and will add sufficient sunshine to a gloomy autumn day.

CLASSIC
EL PRESIDENTE

El Presidente was created in Havana during Prohibition. The exact history of its origin cannot be entirely traced, as is the case for a lot of cocktails. According to some sources, El Presidente was designed by Eddy Woelke, an American bartender who worked at the Jockey Club in Havana. He named his cocktail after Gerardo Machado, the president of Cuba at the time. Others claim that it was named after another Cuban president, namely Mario Garcia. However, it is certain that El Presidente was particularly popular with the upper class.

PREPARATION

Put all the ingredients in a mixing glass, add ice and stir until the required cooling and dilution time have been reached. Strain the cocktail into a precooled cocktail glass and perfume with orange zest.

INGREDIENTS

50 ml (1¾ fl. oz) mature Cuban rum ....
30 ml (1 fl. oz) sweet vermouth ....
1 bar spoon of orange curaçao...
1 bar spoon of grenadine ....
(preferably homemade) ....
orange zest ....

CLASSIC
MOJITO

The mojito cocktail originated on the island of Cuba and is one of the best-known cocktails in the world. However, it also has a disputed history. Some say that the drink was created in 1500, when the explorer Sir Francis Drake was presented with the drink by one of his crew as consolation, because he failed to find any gold in Cuba. Others claim that the mojito was invented by the African slaves who worked at sugar cane plantations. The mojito got a serious boost when Bacardi came to the fore in the middle of the nineteenth century.

The best-known mojito fan was undoubtedly Ernest Hemingway. On the wall of the Cuban bar *Bodeguita Del Medio* he wrote: "My mojito in La Bodeguita, My daiquiri in El Floridita". These words still appear on the bar wall.

The original recipe used sugar cane juice; lime was not added. The mojito as everybody knows it today – the recipe we have given here – is more like a *Queens Park Swizzle* than the original mojito...

INGREDIENTS
50 ml (1¾ fl. oz) white Cuban rum ....
¾ of a lime ....
2 bar spoons of cane sugar ....
8 large mint leaves ....
soda water ....
Angostura bitters ....

PREPARATION
Cut the lime into pieces and place in a long drink glass together with the sugar. Use a muddler to crush and mix the lime and the sugar. Add the mint leaves and crush once again using the muddler. Add the rum and crushed ice and use a bar spoon to mix. Fill up the glass with more crushed ice and top off with soda water. Put a few drops of Angostura bitters on the crushed ice. Garnish with a sprig of mint that has been smacked gently against the palm of your hand. Finish with two straws and enjoy the sun in your glass!

CLASSIC
DAIQUIRI

This cocktail is said to have been created around 1900 at a bar in Santiago, Cuba. According to persistent rumour, an American mining engineer named Jennings Cox created the drink because he had run out of gin, whereas there was plenty of lime and sugar.

The daiquiri began to conquer the world after Admiral W. Johnson introduced the drink to the Army and Navy Club in Washington. Its recipe is based on a *punch rhyme* that was formerly used in the Caribbean: "One of sour, two of sweet, three of strong, four of weak!" *Sweet* stood for the sweetener, *sour* was the acidic flavour, *strong* referred to the alcohol and *weak* was just water, in most cases, to reduce the alcohol level.

PREPARATION

Put all the ingredients in a cocktail shaker, top up with ice and shake until the required cooling time and dilution has been reached (at least 10 seconds!). Strain into a precooled cocktail glass and garnish with a lime wedge.

INGREDIENTS

60 ml (2 fl. oz) white rum ....
20 ml (2/3 fl. oz) fresh lime juice..
20 ml (2/3 fl. oz) of sugar syrup (1 part water to 1 part sugar; use only 10 ml (1/3 fl. oz) for syrup you have bought).............

CLASSIC
RUM OLD FASHIONED

The Old Fashioned is said to have been created between 1889 and 1895 at the Pendennis Club, a gentlemen's club in Louisville, Kentucky. A certain Martin Cuneo created the cocktail for the first time for Colonel James E. Pepper, a prominent bourbon distiller. James enjoyed the drink so much that he introduced it to the Waldorf Astoria in New York. From that moment on things went very well for our classic friend. Originally, this was a drink for which bourbon or American whiskey was used, but those who want to be a little different can replace it with a matured rum of their choice.

PREPARATION

Put the sugar in a tumbler and dissolve it in a bit of soda water. Add the rum and the cocktail bitters and fill up the glass with ice. Stir until the required dilution and cooling time have been reached. Please note: this drink is drunk with ice, so do not stir TOO long as the drink will get diluted further anyway. Perfume and garnish with a bit of orange zest.

INGREDIENTS

50 ml (1¾ fl. oz) mature rum of your choice ....
2 splashes of cocktail bitters .....
1 bar spoon of cane sugar (to taste) ....
orange zest ....

CLASSIC
CUBA LIBRE

According to the legend, Cuba Libre was created in a bar in Havana – how could it be otherwise…? It is said that during the Spanish-American War a captain had accidentally ordered this mixture of cola, rum and lime and his example was followed by quite a lot of soldiers. While they were drinking, they chanted *Cuba Libre* and the name of the cocktail was born. Other sources speak of a more artisanal past, in which a thick syrup of kola nuts and coca leaves was combined with rum and lime. This syrup was allegedly replaced after the introduction of the well-known soft drink in 1900. Cuba Libre had its heyday during the American liberation of Cuba.

PREPARATION

Cut half a lime in two. Fill a long drink glass with ice cubes and squeeze the two lime quarters over the ice. Add the rum, stir and top off with coke.

INGREDIENTS

cola soft drink.............................
50 ml (1¾ fl. oz) white rum ......
half a lime ....

FIVE TIKI COCKTAILS

Tropical beaches, swaying palm trees, exotic beauties, Hawaiian shirts and a seductive hula dance... Tiki cocktails, indeed! Nevertheless, many people could not name a single tiki cocktail. Tiki culture more or less disappeared after about 1980, but today it is experiencing a revival. To fully understand the tiki culture and its fruity and tropical drinks, we have to go back to the United States of the 1930s and the cultural phenomenon that was triggered by tiki at the time.

It all started with a certain Ernest Beamount Gannt, aka Don Beach, and his restaurant, The Beachcomber. His many journeys to the Pacific, mainly Hawaii, had made Don a real connoisseur of Polynesian culture. However, his tiki cocktails were not entirely of Polynesian origin. Don found his inspiration in the Caribbean, where rum, sugar and lime were part of everyday life. Of course, Don did not stick to these ingredients alone, but also started experimenting with various types of rum, home-made syrups, herbal mixtures and fresh juices. His bar was the embodiment of a tropical destination: blazing torches, rattan furniture, exotic cocktails and a dazzling holiday atmosphere. And it was this holiday atmosphere that made his bar extremely popular with the locals and celebrities.

Another well-known name in the American tiki culture was Vic Bergeron, also known as Trader Vic. Vic witnessed the success of The Beachcomber and opened his own tiki restaurant too. Don and Vic were very successful; they both set up proper restaurant chains and are considered the founders of tiki culture. They both also claimed to be the creator of the famous Mai Tai.

Tiki bars became a real trend after the Second World War. Many American soldiers who had fought in the Pacific looked for something that would remind them of that tropical experience and found it in the tiki bars. In any case, Polynesian culture flooded the United States and the associated kitsch was much appreciated. Almost every American town had its own tiki restaurant. Yet by the end of the 1950s, tiki culture in the United States was threatened with extinction. But then Hawaii became a part of the United States and a lot of Americans started holidaying on the tropical island.

The 'tiki high point' followed in the mid-1960s: houses bathed in a tropical atmosphere, the bamboo industry was in its heyday and Hawaiian garden parties were held everywhere... with the associated tiki cocktails, of course. The collapse followed a few years later, during the turbulent end of the 1960s. The war in Vietnam and the conflict between generations meant that the tiki culture died a quiet death. However, one man succeeded in putting tiki cocktails back on the map in the middle of the 1990s. In his book *Grog Log*, Jeff 'Beachbum' Berry revived lost tiki recipes. 'Beachbum' Berry has now published numerous books, which have made him a living legend and probably the most celebrated tiki connoisseur in the world.

Tiki cocktails continue to inspire bars to this day. The mystery surrounding these fantastic drinks undoubtedly makes visiting the bars worthwhile. Tiki cocktails have historically been potent brews and that is how we want to serve them!

TIKI
MAI TAI

This is undoubtedly the best-known tiki cocktail. It was created by Trader Vic. In 1944, he made the drink for two friends from Tahiti. One of those friends, Carrie Guild, then cried out, "Maita'i roa ae!" which means "Out of this world" in Hawaiian. The cocktail became such a hit that the rum used for it, a seventeen-year old 63% Jamaican rum imported by J. Wray & Nephew, was sold out in no time. Vic therefore had to replace the rum with a blend of matured rhum agricole and matured Jamaican rum. Today, only a few bottles of J. Wray & Nephew are left and you will not find one for sale for less than 50,000 euros...

PREPARATION

Put all the ingredients in a cocktail shaker and fill it two thirds full with crushed ice. After shaking hard for ten seconds, you can pour the entire contents into an Old Fashioned glass. Serve with a sprig of mint and half a squeezed lime.

INGREDIENTS

30 ml (1 fl. oz) mature rhum agricole..
30 ml (1 fl. oz) mature Jamaican rum ....
15 ml (½ fl.oz) orange curaçao ....
30 ml (1 fl. oz) fresh lime juice..
15 ml (½ fl. oz) orgeat syrup .....

TIKI
PLANTER'S PUNCH

As the name indicates, this was the punch served by plantation owners. The Planter's Punch is also based on the now familiar punch rhyme. The recipe below is one of the five variants that were found on the menu of Don The Beachcomber in 1937. It perfectly demonstrates Don's complex take on the punch rhyme. Why restrict yourself to one sugar syrup or one type of alcohol, if you can combine to your heart's content and create more complexity? In the days of Don The Beachcomber, the blender was a much used bar instrument and it can still be relevant today if used with the required knowledge and precision.

PREPARATION

Put all the ingredients in a blender and blend for not more than five seconds. Pour the contents into a long drink glass and top up the glass with ice.

Note! *Falernum is one of the many special syrups that you can find in a tiki bar. Recipes can easily be found online. Falernum can be bought in the more up-market drinks shops. John D. Taylor (from the R.L. Seale Distillery) creates a very nice variant.*

INGREDIENTS

15 ml (½ fl. oz) young Jamaican rum ....
15 ml (½ fl. oz) mature Jamaican rum ....
30 ml (1 fl. oz) young Cuban rum...
15 ml (½ fl. oz) fresh lime juice ....
15 ml (½ fl. oz) sugar syrup (1 part sugar to 1 part water) .....
1 bar spoon of grenadine (preferably homemade) ....
1 bar spoon of falernum ....
2 splashes Angostura bitters .....
175 g crushed ice (6 ice cubes)..

TIKI
ZOMBIE

Tiki drinks are notorious for their alcohol content, but this drink went a step further in 1934. If you find it on a menu in a bar, it often states that the maximum per person is two. And that is not a marketing trick. Drink any more and you would qualify for a role in a zombie movie. This drink was also created by Don The Beachcomber and it is his oldest known recipe.

PREPARATION

Put everything in a blender and blend for not more than five seconds. Pour the content into a large long drink glass and top it up with ice cubes. Garnish with a sprig of mint.

INGREDIENTS

45 ml (1½ fl. oz) Puerto Rican rum ....

45 ml (1½ fl. oz) mature Jamaican rum ....

30 ml (1 fl. oz) *overproof* Demerara rum ....

20 ml (⅔ fl. oz) lime juice ....

15 ml (½ fl. oz) Don's Mix (10 ml of white grapefruit juice and 5 ml of cinnamon syrup)

15 ml (½ fl. oz) of falernum...

2 bar spoons of grenadine (preferably homemade) ....

1 splash Angostura bitters......

6 drops pastis ....

175 g crushed ice (6 ice cubes) ....

NAVY GROG

Originally, a grog was a drink of rum and water. This is the variant that was created by – as you can undoubtedly guess – Don The Beachcomber in around 1941. It was just one of his many fun experiments mixing different rums in the same drink. It was allegedly also Frank Sinatra's favourite drink when he visited Don's bar in Hollywood.

PREPARATION

Put all the ingredients in a shaker and shake until the required dilution and cooling time have been reached. Strain in a tumbler and garnish with an ice cone and a straw through it. If you do not have this, then strain into a tumbler over crushed ice and add two thin straws.

INGREDIENTS

30 ml (1 fl. oz) white Puerto Rican rum ....
30 ml (1 fl. oz) mature Jamaican rum ....
30 ml (1 fl. oz) Demerara rum
30 ml (1 fl. oz) honey mix (2 parts honey to 1 part water) ....
20 ml (²/₃ fl. oz) lime juice ....
20 ml (²/₃ fl. oz) grapefruit juice..
20 ml (²/₃ fl. oz) soda water ..

TIKI
PIÑA PARADISE

This recipe comes from Sam Denning's Club Luau in Miami. It shows how other bartenders took over the techniques of Trader Vic and Don The Beachcomber and gave them their own twist.

PREPARATION

Put the ingredients in a blender and blend until the pieces of pineapple have been ground up. Put the contents into a shaker that is half filled with ice, and start shaking. Pour the contents into the hollowed pineapple. Put two straws in and you're ready!

INGREDIENTS

20 ml (²/₃ fl. oz) of young Puerto Rican rum........................

20 ml (²/₃ fl. oz) mature rhum agricole...

15 ml (½ fl. oz) fresh lime juice ....

15 ml (½ fl. oz) white grapefruit juice.............................

15 ml (½ fl. oz) orange juice......

5 ml sugar syrup (1 part sugar to 1 part water) ....

1 splash Angostura bitters..........

6 drops almond essence ....

2 pieces of pineapple, 5 cm³ ......

RUM
AND CIGARS

Rum and cigars are a match made in heaven. Not only do they originate from the same part of the world, but they are also both made to be enjoyed. So why not combine them and double the enjoyment?

What is the key to this ultimate pleasure? Try to find a cigar to balance against the taste of the rum, or to complement it. In other words: use the cigar to enhance certain flavours that can already be found in the rum, or to add subtle flavour accents. That's easier said than done, of course. After all, not everyone is a virtuoso in matters of taste and for all we know you may never even have smoked a cigar. But if you want to take that step, we have one golden tip: go for quality, in both the rum and the cigar.

We have to admit that we're laymen as well when it comes to cigars. That's why we brought in someone for advice: Dominique Gyselinck, the owner of no less than three La Casa del Habano shops, as well as Casa del Tabaco. On top of that, Dominique is one of the very few female cigar sommeliers.

A BRIEF INTRODUCTION

Because this is a book about rum and not cigars, and because we prefer to leave the wonderful world of cigars to the genuine experts, we are not going to give an extensive account about cigars. Nevertheless, we would like to briefly introduce this good friend of our favourite spirit.

SHORT FILLER VERSUS LONG FILLER

As with rum, there are quite a number of varieties of cigars available. Even so, they've all got the same anatomy: the filler, the binder and the wrapper. The wrapper leaf in particular reveals a lot about the quality of the cigar. The colour should be even, there should not be any heavy veins on it, there should be a slight oily sheen and it must be silky soft to the touch.

The filler is rolled up in the surrounding leaf (the binder) and the outer leaf (the wrapper) is then rolled around it. There are two ways in which the interior filler of the cigar can be processed. And this is where you get the difference between a *short filler* and a *long filler*. A short filler has a filling of cut tobacco that is first rolled up in the binder and then in the wrapper. That mixture can consist of a blend of various types of tobacco.

Nowadays, most short fillers are made by machine and are mostly produced in countries where tobacco is not grown. The filler – i.e. the content – of a long filler consists of whole tobacco leaves that are rolled up in the binder. That binder is then finished by having a wrapper rolled around it. Only a few varieties are used for producing these intact tobacco leaves. Long fillers often come from the Caribbean area and Central America and they are rolled by hand.

THE TOBACCO

A premium cigar is made of 100% tobacco and the quality of the tobacco ultimately determines how good a cigar it is. As with wine, the taste and the aroma depend on the terroir.

The tobacco plant originally only grew in tropical and subtropical areas with humid climates, but nowadays it can be cultivated throughout the world. The most common types of tobacco that are used for making cigars come from countries such as Brazil, Cuba, the Dominican Republic, Honduras, Nicaragua, Java and Sumatra.

Superior quality cigar tobacco thrives best around the equator, on volcanic or clay soils rich in humus. When the tobacco plant is mature, after about eighty days, the leaves are plucked, starting from the bottom and working up. The bottom leaves are called 'sand lugs' or 'sand leaves'. Sand lugs yield the best quality and these are therefore mostly used to bind cigars.

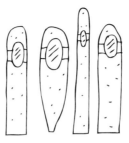

MODELS

There is quite a variety of models within the range of cigars available, each with its own specific characteristics in terms of smoke and taste. In other words, there is a cigar for everybody.

If you like silky smooth, you are better off picking a somewhat thicker shape. The combustion temperature in a thicker cigar is lower and there is less carbonisation. The filler, binder and wrapper are then better in balance as well. That allows a broad aroma to develop. Conversely, the combustion temperature in a thinner cigar is higher, making the taste just a little more potent. There are cigars in a hundred and one different shapes, but we will stick to the seven most common shapes.

CIGARILLO

A slender, lightweight model that is suitable for a brief smoking pause. The cigarillo is modest in diameter, with an aroma somewhere between sharp and soft.

TUITKNAK

This model of cigar is a delight to smoke. It takes about as long to smoke as a señorita but it is a touch less spicy. You light the cigar at the pointed end.

SEÑORITA

This is the most widely smoked type of cigar because it combines the rich aroma of the larger cigars with the shorter smoking time of the smaller models. Perfect for anyone who wants to get acquainted with better types of cigars.

WILD SEÑORITA OR WILD HAVANA

This balanced cigar is a señorita with an uncut end, which gives it a more adventurous image.

PANATELLA

An elegant model whose key feature is that it is relatively long in comparison to its thickness. Popular among women.

ROBUSTO

A popular short, thick cigar, produced in Cuba.

CORONA

The king among cigars and the perfect after-dinner smoke. Coronas have the ideal burning temperature and so are exceptionally smooth. You should take the best part of an hour over one.

SOME USEFUL TIPS!

THE CHOICE

If you have already managed to sample the delights of a cigar, you may already know what type you prefer. But if you're a novice, we have just one recommendation: let someone advise you! Go to a specialist cigar shop, such as La Casa del Habano, with someone who knows what they're talking about and find out what you like and prefer.

CUTTING

Once you have found the perfect cigar, it may need to be cut (depending on the type). This mostly applies to long fillers that have a covered top. Cutting off the head gives you a very fresh piece to draw on.

There are various methods for cutting a cigar. The first method is sometimes called a guillotine cut because the head is cut off just like in a guillotine. Make sure that you don't cut off too large a chunk of the head; you will lose too much of the cigar and risk tearing it. Two less commonly used methods are a

V-cut and making a hole in the middle of the head. The V-cut means making a V-shaped cut in your cigar to leave a smaller opening, thereby giving a more concentrated taste. When making a simple hole, the top cap is essentially twisted off, leaving a neat circular hole to draw the smoke through. Again, we recommend having an expert with you the first time.

LIGHTING UP

The way in which a cigar is lit has a major influence on the taste and the way the cigar burns. The rule here is "more haste, less speed"... hurrying won't work. Use a butane lighter, a long match or a wooden spill. If you use a match, wait until the head has burned away, because the chemicals will ruin the taste of your cigar. Hold the cigar above the flame and turn it round slowly. Never put the cigar directly in the flame. Once the very end is evenly glowing red, draw in small puffs and blow gently on the glowing end.

SMOKING

You will get the best out of a cigar if you smoke it calmly. Savour or taste the smoke by taking small puffs. Let the smoke rest in the mouth and take your time to

enjoy all the taste impressions. The cigar will get too hot if you go too quickly, losing its subtle taste and becoming bitter. The taste may change over the course of smoking it. There is a turning point about halfway through: the cigar loses its soft taste and acquires a stubborn and unruly side. When to stop smoking the cigar is entirely up to you, but it will probably be when you are about two-thirds through it.

TAPPING THE ASH OFF OR NOT

A premium cigar creates a long tip of ash. Some smokers enjoy deliberately creating a long cylinder of ash. There are no rules for this and everyone has their own preferences, so tapping the ash off is perfectly okay. It is sometimes claimed that the ash on the end has a cooling effect that improves the taste of a cigar. If you want to relight a cigar that has been put out – even though there is often no pleasure left in a cigar that has been half smoked – don't hold it between your lips.

PUTTING THE CIGAR OUT

Never press a cigar down to put it out – let it go out quietly of its own accord.

THE CIGAR BAND

The cigar band or label was used in Europe for protecting the wrapper leaf while smoking the cigar. In America, however, the band showed how far a cigar could be smoked. These were initially blank strips of paper and only later were they printed with logos and used for decorating the whole package. But what should you do with this band? Actually it's very easy: just leave it there, around the cigar. If you try to take it off before smoking, it might make a hole in the wrapper that would make the cigar draw less well. The band often loosens a bit while the cigar is being smoked and you can then carefully remove it.

STORAGE

When it comes to storing cigars, we make a clear distinction between long fillers and short fillers. Short fillers are best kept at a humidity of about 40%, whereas long fillers need a relative humidity of 65%-70% and temperatures of between 16°C-18°C. A long filler has to be resilient and therefore needs to be smoked shortly after being purchased, within a couple of days at most. If you want to keep long fillers for longer, then you should consider acquiring a humidor.

"If I ever go missing, please put my photo on a rum bottle, not a milk carton. I want my friends to know I am missing!"

Laurie Manzer, *American anti-police activist*

LET'S PAIR UP!

After this brief introduction, it's now time for the real work. Pairing up rum and cigars – double the pleasure! Find a special moment with someone whose company you enjoy and let the magic do its work.

We have selected six rums and Dominique Gyselinck has picked two matching cigars for each. The rums are a matured and non-matured version in the English, French or Spanish style each time.

SPANISH STYLE

DICTADOR 100 CLARO +
HOYO DE MONTERREY EPICURE NO. 2
OR DAVIDOFF ENTREACTO

The Cuban Epicure has everything a connoisseur could desire. Soft and creamy, with notes of cedar that combine perfectly with the buttery taste of the Dictador Claro rum. The vanilla and coffee edges of the rum complement the cedar notes of the cigar beautifully. The Davidoff Entreacto with its Dominican filler and aromas of leather and cedar wood goes fantastically with the Dictador 100 Claro.

DIPLOMÁTICO RESERVA EXCLUSIVA +
ROMEO Y JULIETA NO. 2 TUBO
OR DAVIDOFF CLASSIC LINE

The Diplomático Reserva Exclusiva with its tastes of caramel, cocoa and a hint of nut goes perfectly with the soft Romeo y Julieta from Cuba with its woody overtones. A classic Davidoff also pairs up fantastically with this rum.

ENGLISH STYLE

PLANTATION 3 STARS +
PARTAGAS SERIES D NO. 4
OR DAVIDOFF CAMACHO COROJO

The Partagas Robusto is perhaps the best robusto in the world. Within it you will taste rich and powerful exotic wood aromas, alternating with notes of leather and pepper. In turn, the Davidoff Camacho Corojo comes from Honduras and is powerful and slightly bitter, leaving a mocha taste in the throat. Both cigars are excellent with Plantation 3 Stars, with its aroma of tropical fruit and a rich taste of banana, coconut, mandarin oranges and butterscotch.

PUSSER'S 15 YEARS NAVY RUM +
BOLIVAR BELICOSSO
OR DAVIDOFF LIMITED EDITION 2015
YEAR OF THE SHEEP

Pusser's 15 Years is a rum with a deep aroma of dark sugar and wood. The taste is full of spiciness and brown sugar, as well as notes of cinnamon, vanilla, light wood and cloves. The Cuban Bolivar Belicosso is a fresh and potent cigar with a bitter taste that has touches of citrus. It is the perfect counterweight to the spicy rum. The Davidoff Limited Edition 2015 Year of the Sheep has a peppery taste, with bitter aromas and a touch of cedar, perfectly complementing the rum.

FRENCH STYLE

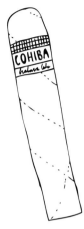

TROIS RIVIÈRES CUVÉE DE L'OCÉAN + COHIBA SIGLO VI OR RAMON ALLONES SPECIALLY SELECTED

The Cuban Cohiba is a sweet cigar that tastes of white chocolate. Velvety soft in the mouth, with a note of cedar. The Ramon, which also comes from Cuba, has more of a herbal taste, full and woody. The salty edge and herbal taste of the Trois Rivières Cuvée are a perfect match for both cigars.

CLÉMENT VSOP + DAVIDOFF PURO D'ORO OR FONESCA BENELUX EDITION

Clément VSOP has an aroma of oranges, apples and a touch of other vegetal flavours. The taste is spicy, slightly smoky and herbal, with a hint or roasted almonds and walnuts. The Davidoff Puro d'Oro has a Dominican background and it is the brand's luxury product. It is soft, sweet, rich and velvety in the mouth. In turn, the Fonesca is rather sweet, with hints of gingerbread and cedar. Together with the Clément VSOP, both cigars will be a delight.

8 MUST-VISIT BARS

THE DRIFTER

BELGIUM – GHENT

WWW.THEDRIFTER.BE

Belgium got its first permanent tiki bar in 2014! The Drifter in the Oudburg district of Ghent is the brainchild of Tom Neijens... Indeed, one of the authors of this book! Tom's vast enthusiasm and love of the job have helped him create a southern ambience in The Drifter. The bar specialises in tiki cocktails, of course, with a personal twist if you want. The selection of rums is absolutely mouth-watering. The ever-growing collection of over 150 rums contains some unusual variants that you won't be able to find anywhere else. The impressive selection of rums is not the only reason for making a detour to The Drifter: the interior is great too, with tiki pictures, floral wreaths, bamboo, wooden masks and so forth. All the ingredients are there to help you forget the sometimes awful Belgian weather outside. And Tom's cocktails are of course fantastic.

DIRTY DICK

FRANCE – PARIS
HTTP://ON.FB.ME/1Q9SDEX

Dirty Dick is in the edgy but ultra-trendy SoPi – South Pigalle – district of Paris. A genuine tiki bar that is a perfect blend of bar and club. Dirty Dick is a reference to the brothel that was located in the building from 1931 until just a few years ago. The hipster barmen in equally trendy shirts shake the tastiest tiki cocktails, with evocative names such as the Cannibal's Dilemma, the Zombie or Don the Beachcomber. In other words, this is where you go for superb cocktails in which rum plays the leading role. Or if you'd prefer the pure version, that's no problem: Dirty Dick has around 140 types of rum. And the layout? Exotic kitsch with a tongue-in-cheek dash of Hawaii Five-O.

BABA AU RUM

GREECE - ATHENS
WWW.BABAAURUM.COM

Since it was founded in 2009, Baba Au Rum has maintained its high standards in service and drinks with consistency and professionalism. To this day it is still a global reference to post-Tiki era rum bars. It was the bar that started everything in what is now one of the most vibrant bar scenes around the world. It is no coincidence that most of the very best Greek bartenders used to work there. Thanos Prunarus, the founder, owner and manager, is also a bartender with twenty years' experience. Baba Au Rum has been awarded three times as one of the World's 50 Best Bars (2013, 2016 and 2017). Its cocktail menu was on the Top 10 shortlist of Tales of the Cocktail in the World's Best Menus category, the bar itself on the Top 10 short list for World's Best High Volume Bars category. Its well-executed side projects (Rum Festival, the Fine magazine, the Mary Pickford Bar etc.) have fuelled the bar's international fame, bringing more rum aficionados together and getting them to visit Athens and choose Baba Au Rum as one of their worldwide favourites.

NU LOUNGE BAR

ITALY - BOLOGNA
WWW.NULOUNGEBAR.COM

Nu Lounge Bar is where you can enjoy the most sophisticated cocktails in a breathtaking Italian interior with tall trees and walls that are decorated with frescoes. Nu Lounge Bar is the 'laboratory' of Daniele Dalla Pola, one of the world's most renowned 'mixologists'. In 2011 he was crowned world champion at the *Below Cocktail World Cup* in New Zealand. Drawing his inspiration from Polynesian mythology, he shakes up some genuine tiki masterpieces. Daniele is an Italian master in creating cocktails that suit the client's mood. You will have no trouble at all spending the whole evening here – or all night! The moment you come in the door, you'll think you're in exotic lands.

TAFIA

JAPAN - TOKYO
WWW.TAFIA.JP

Tafia has Japan's largest collection of rhum agricole and the bartenders pride themselves on serving original tiki cocktails. You can enjoy more than 300 kinds of rum, accompanied by typical Caribbean recipes. Tafia's owner is a member of the board of R.U.M. Japan (Rum Union Members Japan), a group that looks to promote rum in Japan by holding all kinds of seminars and events, as well as making efforts to introduce a rum classification system. Tafia is happy to welcome both seasoned rum lovers and complete novices.

TRAILER HAPPINESS

UNITED KINGDOM - LONDON
WWW.TRAILERHAPPINESS.COM

Trailer Happiness is a lounge and tiki bar on Portobello Road in the heart of London. It is famous for its fantastic music and cocktails. Trailer Happiness is the home base of the Notting Hill Rum Club and it has a collection of more than 200 rums. They serve both classic and modern cocktails, all with a *tiki twist*. The interior is kitsch, with dark walls lit up with colourful elements. The bar is the favourite hot spot for numerous celebrities, both local and from further afield. During the week you can usually get in without a reservation, but you will need to book at the weekend.

SMUGGLER'S COVE

UNITED STATES – SAN FRANCISCO
WWW.SMUGGLERSCOVESF.COM

Smuggler's Cove is sure to make the heart of any rum aficionado beat a little faster. This rum and tiki bar has about 600 variants – this being the biggest collection of rums in the United States, including some very rare bottles from the nineteenth century. The cocktails that are served perfectly reflect the three-century-old history of rum and rum cocktails. When you go inside, it's as if you are down in the belly of a ship, decorated with all kinds of ropes, fishing gear, lanterns and old rum bottles. It is the complete rum experience, not to mention the fun you'll have there too!

TACOMA CABANA

UNITED STATES – TACOMA
WWW.TACOMACABANA.COM

Tacoma Cabana opened in 2012. The people running it drew their inspiration from the Okolemaluna Tiki Lounge in Hawaii. They say they were so overwhelmed by the concept that they decided to open their own temple for exotic drinks. The interior has been carefully thought out; Murphy and Alexander spent months collecting all kinds of fun tiki items. In 2016, this tiki bar had more than 300 kinds of rum and a cocktail menu that deserves serious respect. You can also enjoy a number of great 'holiday dishes' there.

ALPHABETICAL INDEX

SOURCES

AYALA, LUIS K., *The rum experience*, 2001.
BERRY J., *Potions of the Caribbean*, 2013.
WILLIAMS I., *Rum, a social and sociable history*, 2008.

www.plantationrum.com
www.rumbarrel.com
www.eater.com
www.wikipedia.org
www.cigarswithrum.blogspot.be
www.sigarologie.nl
www.cigars4dummies.com

COLOPHON

WWW.LANNOO.COM

Register with our website and we'll send you a regular newsletter with information about new books and interesting exclusive offers.

Text
Isabel Boons & Tom Neijens
Editing
Katrien Meuleman, Clare Wilkinson
Translation
Mike Wilkinson, Ruud Faulhaber

Photography
Wim Kempenaers, with the exception of p. 10 © New Grove Rum, p. 20 Tratong/Shutterstock, pp. 30-31 Sapsiwai/Shutterstock, p. 37 Apollofoto/Shutterstock, p. 42 © New Grove Rum, pp. 46-47 Johan Larson/Shutterstock, p. 52 © New Grove Rum, p. 54 Kishivan/Shutterstock, p. 60 Dima Sobko/Shutterstock, p. 66 Jozef Sowa/Shutterstock, p. 74 Natali Zakharova/Shutterstock, p. 344 Jag_cz/Shutterstock, p. 384 Filipe Frazao/Shutterstock, p. 388 The Drifter, p. 389 Dirty Dick, p. 390 Baba au Rum, p. 391 Nu Lounge Bar, p. 392 Tafia, p. 393 Trailer Happiness, p. 394 Smuggler's Cove, p. 395 Tacoma Cabana

Illustrations
Emma Thyssen

Design
Kiet

Layout
Asterisk*, Amsterdam

If you have any remarks or questions, please contact our editors: redactiestijl@lannoo.com.

© LANNOO PUBLISHERS, 2018

D/2018/45/48 – NUR 447

ISBN: 978 94 014 5007 2

All rights reserved. No part of this publication may be replicated, stored in an automated retrieval system and/or published, in any form or by any means, whether electronically, mechanically or in any other manner, without the prior written permission of the publisher.